Contents

[v]

Contents

[vi]

Contents

The Mystery of Golf

"...ces jeux où se mêlent merveilleusement, pour interroger notre fortune, le hasard et la science; jeux presque mystiques et toujours passionnants, où l'homme se plaît à tâter sa chance aux confins de son être."

MAURICE MAETERLINCK

THE MYSTERY
OF GOLF

Proem

THREE things there are as un-
fathomable as they are fascinating to the masculine mind:
metaphysics; golf; and the fem- *The writer is*
inine heart. The Germans, I believe, pre- *astonied at*
tend to have solved some of the riddles of *the mysterie*
the first, and the French to have unravelled *of the game*
some of the intricacies of the last; will some *ycleped*
one tell us wherein lies the extraordinary *golfe;*
fascination of golf?

I have just come home from my Club.
We played till we could not see the flag; the
caddies were sent ahead to find the balls by
the thud of their fall; and a low large moon

threw whispering shadows on the dew-wet grass or ere we trode the home-green. At dinner the talk was of golf; and for three mortal hours after dinner the talk was — of golf. Yet the talkers were neither idiots, *And eke the* fools, nor monomaniacs. On the contrary, *zeale which* many of them were grave men of the *yt evoketh.* world. At all events the most monomaniacal of the lot was a prosperous man of affairs, worth I do not know how many thousands, which thousands he had made by the same mental faculties by which this evening he was trying to probe or to elucidate the profundities and complexities of this so-called "game." Will some one tell us wherein lies its mystery?

I

He confesseth I AM a recent convert to golf. But it is the re-*his ignorance* cent convert who most closely scrutinizes *thereof;* his creed — as certainly it is the recent convert who most zealously avows it. The old to suggest that a small portion of the links might be set apart for a court—the turf about the home-hole was very tempting. The dead silence with which this innocent proposition was received gave him pause. (He sees now that an onlooker might as well have requested from a whist party the loan of a few cards out of the pack to play card-tricks withal.)

Yet it is neither incomprehensible nor ir-rational, this misconception on the part of the layman of the royal and antient game of golf. To the uninitiated, what is there in golf to be seen? A ball driven of a club; that is all. There is no exhibition of skill opposed to skill or of strength contending with strength; there is apparently no prow-ess, no strategy, no tactics—no pitting of muscle and brain against muscle and brain. At least, so it seems to the layman. When the layman has caught the infection, he thinks—and knows—better.

Yet he admit-teth that he may err;

As many an other hath erred.

But, as a matter of fact, contempt could be poured upon any game by anyone unacquainted with that game. We know with what apathetic contempt Subadar Chinniah or Jemadar Mohamed Khan looks on while Tommy Atkins swelters as he bowls or bats or fields under a broiling Indian sun, or Tommy's subalterns kick up the maidan's dust with their polo-ponies' hoofs. And what could be more senseless to a being wholly ignorant of cards than the sight of four grey-headed men gravely seating themselves before dinner to arrange in certain artificial combinations certain uncouth pictures of kings and queens and knaves and certain spots of red and black? Not until such a being recognizes the infinite combinations of chance and skill possible in that queen of sedentary games does he comprehend the fascination of whist. And so it is with golf. All that is requisite in golf, so it seems to the onlooker, is to hit; and than a

The Layman's Ignorance

"hit" nothing, surely, can be simpler or easier—so simple and easy that to have a
dozen sticks to hit with, and to hire a boy to
carry them, is not so much a sign of pitiable
insanity as of wilful stupidity. The puerility
of the proceeding is enough to make the
spectator irate. Especially as, owing to the *Nathelesse,*
silence and the seriousness with which the *golfe doth*
golfer plays, and his reticence as to the se- *verilie contain*
cret of the game—for none knows better *matter for*
than the golfer that the game renders up its *moche*
secret only to the golfer, if even to him— *puzzlement.*
this quiet, red-coated individual is surrounded with a sort of halo of superiority, a
halo not made by himself. No wonder the
onlooker's anger is aroused. That expert-
ness in puerility of this sort should of itself
exalt a man, make him possessed of that
which obviously, yet unintentionally, raises
him above the intelligent yet indignant on-
looker—there is something in this past
finding out. Nor does he find it out till he

[7]

himself is converted. Golf is like faith: it is the substance of things hoped for, the evidence of things not seen; and not until it is personally experienced does the unbelieving change from the imprecatory to the precatory attitude.

The writer essayeth the game.

However, the erstwhile aforesaid non-playing member of the golf club in question, the suppleness of his epiphyses, it may be, becoming (perhaps not quite imperceptibly) unequal to the activity and agility demanded of them by more ardent games, purchased, first one club, then another, then a sheaf, and betook himself to the task of finding out *a posteriori*, by the experimental method, what there was in the confounded game that brought the players there by scores to play.—And to talk of their play. For it should be added that the talk at that club puzzled him as much as the play. It was not enough that keen King's Counsel, grave judges, erudite men of letters, statesmen, and shrewd men of business should play as if the end of life were to hole a ball; but they talked as if the way a ball should be holed were the only knowledge worth possessing. Well, he played; or, to be more precise, he attempted to play, and, fortunately for him, he persevered in the attempt. Then indeed did the scales fall from his eyes. He discovered that there was more in golf than met the eye — much more.

II

How great a similarity there is in all outdoor human games! Probably ninety per cent. of human outdoor games consist in the propulsion of a spherical or spheroidal object towards a certain spot. In cricket, rounders, football, baseball, polo, basketball, croquet, marbles, tennis, racquets, quoits, billiards, bagatelle, fives, pool, curling, lacrosse, hockey, ping-pong, golf, either one party assails with a ball, a sphere, a

Of human gamys in generall.

spheroid, or a disc a position defended by another, or both parties assail with a similar object the selfsame position, victory lying with the party reaching it first. It would be interesting to dive into the primæval origin of games and to discuss whether the first distinct differentiation of the man from the ape consisted not in the ability to throw a stone and wield a bough, to attack with a sphere and defend with a stick, the pithecanthropoid prototypes of batting and bowling. The first ape that tried to possess himself of a fruit he could not reach, or to repel a foe he could not grapple, by throwing a stone or using a branch, was in all probability the progenitor of the human race. It may, indeed, be that man's erect posture was gradually evolved by this attempt to throw and wield (which could not be done on all fours), and that the ape became the true ἄνθρωπος—the true "face-up-turning" animal *(ἀνὰ — πρέπω — ὤψ)* —

when he succeeded in hurling and hitting. In the case of this supposititious ape, the throwing and hitting were actions primarily prompted by hunger or love, by the desire to obtain food or by the desire to obtain a mate (or to keep off a rival)—the two primal instincts of life. In so far they were highly utilitarian.

With all due deference to Schiller and to Herbert Spencer, with their theory of the "play instinct" as at the bottom of all art, I contend that all our amusements, like all our art, derive ultimately from the most serious, most utilitarian instincts. In the world of life, mere play, *quâ* play, is as non-existent as, in the world of nature, is mere beauty, *quâ* beauty. Beauty is but the perfection of useful matter. The most lovely landscape is but hills and dales and trees. The most wonderful human body is but bone and muscle and fascia and nerve. There is nothing in nature, and there is nothing in the anatomi-

Animadversions uponne certaine theories.

cal frame, put there for beauty's sake alone. All is for use; nothing for ornament. And as art is but the reproduction, the representation, of the perfection of useful nature, so sport is but a reproduction, the representation of the perfection of useful occupation. Even the gambols of kittens and puppies are the hereditary and instinctive reproduction of contests with teeth or claws. In this sense only, in piping times of peace, when man was not afraid of his fellow-man, can man be said to have "played" with his fellow-man — contended with him in amicable and imitative combat. — They are near akin, are art and sport; the one being the intellectual and emotional, the other the muscular and nervous, representation of the primal and highly utilitarian instincts of hunger and love exerting themselves, in the form of hunting and mating and fighting, in a world of animal and vegetable life.

Arte and sporte, they bin neare akin.

All   masculine   games   are   contests.

THE ORIGIN OF GAMES

Whether there are any such things as femi- *Of pass-*
nine games proper is doubtful. When girls *times*
play games they play with their brothers, or *puellile.*
they play their brothers' games. And even
when they play among themselves, their
games prove the evolutionary law, and show
themselves to be refinements on primæval
feminine occupations: they play at "doll's-
house," at "school," at "mistress and maid";
they pay visits to one another, they dress up
in their elders' clothes, they make mud-pies,
they erect diminutive domiciles, they nurse
unheeding dolls. Of these the derivation is
obvious.

One other species of games there is, but *Of hasardrie.*
as into it little or no element of sport enters,
it needs not to be classified here. To gamble
is perhaps as primæval an instinct as to
fight. Herr Karl Groos, indeed, regards
gambling as a sort of fight against fate. In
almost all games, too, an element of chance
inheres—inheres, and thus perhaps en-

hances the interest of the game. But it is a question whether a game of mere and sheer chance deserves the name. Rouge et Noir is hardly a "game"; a sport it certainly is not.

Golfe likened wyth other gamys.

You can detect national character in games. Golf is preëminently the game of the Scot: slow, sure, quiet, deliberate, canny even — each man playing for himself. There is no defensive play, no attacking an enemy's position, no subordination of oneself to the team, no captain to be obeyed, no relative positions of players. Compare with it cricket, the game typical of the Anglo-Saxon of more southern proclivities. Here you have more excitement, greater rapidity of action. There is no serious and contemplative addressing of yourself to the ball; no terrible anxiety over your stance; no forty-two rules for your slog. Golf, on the other hand, is self-reliant, silent, sturdy. It leans less on its fellows. It loves best to overcome obstacles alone. If the golfer take a caddie, it but proves him a member of a clan: his caddie is his fellow-clansman. Of the two, perhaps cricket is for youth the superior game. It requires as keen an eye, as accurate an adjustment of hand and eye, as great muscular power in the stroke, and it is more rapid. It must be played, too, as much as golf, "with the heid." In cricket you have an ally or allies, both in batting and fielding; it is communistic, political. The nation that evolved cricket evolved the British constitution.

Note, too, an you will, the nomenclature proper to golf. Where your blunt and careless Southron cricketer "slogs" or "blocks" or is "stumped," your Northern golfing precisian religiously takes his "stance," "addresses" himself to the ball, and "approaches" the hole;—a phraseology that smacks of the Assembly of Divines. There is something Puritanically and Sinaitically threatening in the thought of "approach- *Of the appellatiouns atte golfe.*

ing" a hole; as if, puir aperture, it were not to be come at but after due preparation thereunto, and were altogether fenced off from the ignorant, the scandalous, and the profane. And so indeed it is: the hole is an ominous and portentous ordinance, and often mightily inconveniently placed; and the duffer who thinks to enter therein without much searching of heart, without diligent use of all means suitable and answerable unto so high and serious a task, if he doth not thereby render himself liable to admonishment by his elders, is nevertheless, in the matter of the "approach," still in the eenfancy of golf!

III

How sporte now be verray prevalaunt.

THERE is rampant in the world at the present moment a sort of sporting mania, an international sporting mania; excellent in its way, but very difficult to analyse or account for. Manias of one kind or another are not unknown to history. Such, for example, was *Whilom* the mania for Crusades in the Middle Ages. *analogues* It had a highly rational basis, namely the *thereto:* defence of Christendom against Islam and the wresting of the Holy Land from its des- *Ye Crusades;* ecrating possessors. But to such lengths did this mania go that in 1212 an army of chil- dren once actually set out, with banners and paraphernalia, to conquer some vague, invisible foe; with the result that hundreds died before they had gone any distance, and hundreds were sold into slavery. Such, too, was the Hippodrome mania in the fourth *Byzantine* century at Byzantium, when feeling ran so *factiouns;* high that society was divided into hostile sections, and money, and even blood, was recklessly spent in contests between the fac- tion of the Green and the faction of the Blue. And such was the tulip mania of *Doutche* Holland in 1637, when, so keen was the ri- *tulyppes.* valry for bulbs, that a whole nation was ab- sorbed in the strife and many a family

ruined itself by speculation in rare or myth-
ical roots.

How folk to-
daye do vye
with these.

Well, to-day the western world seems to
be labouring under something of the same
sort. Year by year athletics occupy a larger
share of the attention, not only of the students, but of the teachers, at our schools
and colleges, and year by year the sums
spent in intercollegiate and international
contests increase. To win a comparatively
valueless cup by means of a comparatively
unserviceable craft, a single individual
spends some millions of sesterces, and two
nations look on intent on the race and applaud. Teams without number, of all kinds,
cross and re-cross the Atlantic and Pacific;
money is poured out like water on race-
horses, motor-cars, dirigible balloons, and
what-not. — Like the Crusades, there is for
all this a highly rational basis, that most
laudable one of amicable rivalry in brain or
muscle; but, like the Crusades, it is a ques-

tion whether it is not here and there just a
little overdone.

IV

AND yet, why is it, let us ask ourselves, that *Of prowesse*
mankind consents to hold prowess in sport *in sporte:*
in such high esteem? From the days of the
Olympian and Isthmian games to the latest
broken record, always athletic excellence
has elicited spontaneous admiration. To the
champion, to him who excels in any kind of
game,—the batsman, the oarsman, the
boxer,—we look up with a certain sort of
awe, an instinctive and mysterious sort of
worship. The feeling is deep-seated and
universal; it must have its roots far down in
the primitive foundations of human history
and human nature.

Well, if my theory that all sport is but *Its founte &*
amicable combat is correct, prowess in *origine;*
games is proof and symbol of prowess in
that inevitable and sempiternal combat of

man with man and of man with nature
without which neither would mankind as
a whole have evolved, nor would special
races of men have emerged and dominated
the world. Men seem instinctively to understand that to excel in strength or agility
means much more than possession of mere
And eke its strength or agility; that it means staying-
explicatioun. power, will, determination, courage—a
host of, not only muscular, but mental and
even moral qualities. It was with quite serious, though perhaps shapeless, motives, that
the Greeks erected statues to their Olympian victors; motives identical probably
with those that led to the deification of Her-
akles and Thor and all the strong men of
mythology.

Of What may be the particular weapon
weaponnes. wielded by the champion matters little,
whether bat or ball, boxing-glove, driver, or
oar. The weapon is but the medium of his
strength and skill, the vehicle of his thought

he has not yet learned everything. He discovers that the character of his opponent and the quality of his opponent's play exercise a most extraordinary influence over him. Does he go out with a greater duffer than himself, unconsciously he finds himself growing over-confident or careless. Does he go out with a redoubtable player, one whose name on the Club Handicap stands at Scratch, he cannot allay a certain exaltation or trepidation highly noxious to his game. And it is in vain that he attempts to reason these away. Not only so, but even after months of practice, when the exaltation or trepidation is under control, often it will happen that an opponent's idiosyncrasies will so thoroughly upset him that he will vow never to play with that idiosyncratic again. This we may call the social or moral element. It affects the feelings or the emotions; it affects the mind through these feelings or emotions; and, through the mind, it affects the muscles.

Now, I take it that there is no other game in which these three fundamental factors—

In this three-folden divisioun golfe proveth itselfe unique.

the physiological, the psychological, and the social or moral—are so extraordinarily combined or so constantly called into play. Some sports, such as football, polo, rowing, call chiefly for muscular activity, judgment, and nerve; others, such as chess, draughts, backgammon, call upon the intellect only. In no other game that I know of is, first, the whole anatomical frame brought into such strenuous yet delicate action at every stroke; or, second, does the mind play so important a part in governing the actions of the muscles; or, third, do the character and temperament of your opponent so powerfully affect you as they do in golf. To play well, these three factors in the game must be most accurately adjusted, and their accurate adjustment is as difficult as it is fascinating.

GOLF AND LIFE

VI

ALL true games, I have said, are contests.
But in golf the contest is not with your fellow-man. The foe in golf is not your oppo- *Golfe likened*
nent, but great Nature herself, and the *unto Lyfe.*
game is to see who will over-reach her better, you or your opponent. In almost all
other games you pit yourself against a mortal foe; in golf it is yourself against the
world: no human being stays your progress
as you drive your ball over the face of the
globe. It is very like life in this, is golf. Life is
not an internecine strife. We are all here
fighting, not against each other for our lives,
but against Nature for our livelihoods. In
golf we can see a symbol of the history and
fate of human kind: careering over the face
of this open earth, governed by rigid rule,
surrounded with hazards, bound to subdue
Nature or ere we can survive, punished for
the minutest divergence from the narrow

course, and the end of it all.... And the end of it all?... To reach an exiguous grave with as few mistakes as may be—some with high and brilliant flight, others with slow and lowly crawl....

VII

To descend, however, from this highly abstract plane, why is it, let us ask, that golf to so many of us seems to-day a game unique?

Well, amongst other things, it is unique because it is so difficult. Curiously enough, its chief difficulty arises from its chief simplicity. In golf you hit a stationary ball. At first blush that sounds the acme of ease. It is not; though it takes even a zealot some days to plumb the depths of that paradox. At first blush it would seem that a cricket ball— flying towards you, its trajectory foreshortened, its velocity variable, its pitch problematical, its break uncertain—would be of all balls the hardest to hit; and the next hardest, seemingly, would be the racquet or the tennis ball. All three come fast, and you never know exactly whence they are coming or whither they are going. The difficulties in cricket, racquets, and tennis seem immense. Yet they are not as great as the difficulties in golf. If they were, we should surely ere this have been, in this analytical era, inundated with theoretic lucubrations as to how these should be played, as assuredly we have been in the matter of golf. Besides, no cricketer *As compayred* suffers agonies in debating with himself of *with kindred* the correctness of his stance, or of the char- *gamys.* acter of his swing; or addresses himself with painful pause to the bowling; or waggles his implement with serious, not to say solemn, insistence; or devoutly locks up a pet bat against the day of some extra-important match; or requires from all spectators of his play the most awesome and reverential silence. What is there in the game of golf which so differentiates it from all others that in it these trifling minutiæ become magnified to matters of great moment? I take it it is because in golf the *mind* plays a highly curious and important part. In cricket, tennis, racquets, polo, the entire absence of such maxims as "Keep your eye on the ball," "Be up," "Slow back," "Follow through," "Don't go to sleep," and the rest of them—all addressed to the mind—shows that in these the mind requires no external or adventitious stimulus. Who would dream of taking his eye off an approaching ball in cricket? —who could do it? Who could possibly go to sleep in the midst of a rally in tennis? Evidently in these games the movement of the ball is sufficient stimulus in itself—it is *the* stimulus. Now, in golf there is no such stimulus, and the mind has to be goaded into attention and action by laborious and incessant iteration of mental formulæ dinned into the memory and repeated over and

Injunctiouns queint & curious.

over again. (I know a man who repeats to
himself six rules every time he takes his
driver in hand and addresses the ball.) This
is curious, but it is true; and perhaps the fol-
lowing train of reasoning will substantiate
the assertion. No game can be played with- *Psychologi-*
out accurate and delicate adjustment of *call explica-*
hand and eye; this adjustment is primarily *tioun.*
the function, through the nerves, of the
mind; it cannot be achieved unless the mind
is instantly and constantly stimulated to action; in all rapid games the movement of
the ball supplies this stimulus, for it excites
the perceptive faculties, and, through them,
the conceptive, by which the orders for the
next stroke are issued; in golf there is little
or no excitation of the perceptive faculties;
accordingly the conceptive faculties have to
be concentrated and roused to action by
artful and adventitious means, by precepts
learned by rote and forcibly applied at every
stroke. That is the psychology of golf. In all

quick games, so strong and so rapid are the stimuli that the resulting movements might almost be called reflex or automatic. Volleying at the net in tennis might certainly be so called: there is no time to think; the very sight of the approaching ball throws the right arm into position to receive and strike it. To the expert tennis-player the movement is doubtless reflex and automatic, as automatic as the closing of the eyelid on the approach of a fly—though both, probably, are the result of constant response to stimulus. Now, in golf there is never any reflex action possible. Every stroke must be played by the mind—gravely, quietly, deliberately. And this is why there is a psychology of golf but there is no psychology of cricket or racquets or tennis or polo. If for this theory it is necessary to show that strong stimulation of the perceptive faculties tends to strong stimulation of the conceptive, one might point to the effect of music upon the mind and body. How easy it is to dance when the rhythmic valse strikes upon the ear! what waves of thought and emotion are set agoing at sound of martial airs!

VIII

As a matter of fact most of the difficulties in golf are mental, not physical; are subjective, not objective; are the created phantasms of the mind, not the veritable realities of the course. Bad lies, on good links, are the exception, not the rule; and bunkers are avowedly where they are in order to catch the unworthy and the unwary. That wood to the right is no real obstacle to your drive; why then are you so fearful of a slice? Were you blindfold and could not see it, it would be as if it were not, and the so-called "difficulty" would vanish. And yet the number of balls that do go into that wood — or are pulled off to the left to avoid it — is aston-

The chiefest difficulties, they be more fantastical than reall.

ishing. — The mere test of strength or of skill is one of the most subordinate of the elements of golf; much more important is the test of what goes by the name of "nerve," that quiet self-confidence which no ghostly phantasms can shake, in howsoever questionable shape they come. So many golfers forget this. "If I had not done this, that, or the other stupid thing," they say, "my score would have been so-and-so." My dear sir, it is just those stupid things that make the game. Eliminate the liability of the frail and peccant human mind to do stupid things, and you might as well play pitch and toss. It is this very frailty and peccability of the human mind that golf calls in question, and it is this that differentiates golf from all other games, because in golf this frailty is shown in its utter nudity, not hidden away under cover of agility or excitement or concerted action, as it is in cricket or football or tennis or polo or what-not.

'Tis human frailtie that golfe yt putteth to ye teste.

The Difficulty Subjective

The simplicity of the thing to be done strips the soul of all cloak of excuse for not doing it. You may place your ball how or where you like, you may hit it with any sort of implement you like; all you have to do is to hit it into a hole. Could simpler conditions be devised? Could an easier task be essayed? And yet, such is the extraordinary constitution of the human golfing soul, that it not only fails to achieve it, but invents for itself multiform and manifold ifs and ans for not achieving it: ifs and ans the nature and number of which must assuredly move the laughter of the gods.... I have often thought that golf was the invention of the de — well, let us say, of the deities of Olympus, an invention contrived for a twofold purpose: first to afford them subject-matter for merriment; and second to prove to vaunting man how trivial a creature he is. —In my mind's eye I can see brawny Zeus, with stout Hera at his side (she must be in-

Golfe a sighte for the goddes.

clining to *embonpoint* by this time), lying beside his nectar and watching puny men chasing pigmy balls over this paltry planet. What inextinguishable laughter must ring through the Sacred Mount at sight of grave statesmen and puissant potentates, mighty satraps and great pro-consuls, Right Reverends and Right Honourables, striving strenuously to put little pieces of india-rubber into little holes in the ground, and "damnin' awfu'" when they don't!...

IX

Howbeit, the cadet and the professioun-all, it needeth not that they doe analyse their playe.

HOWEVER, probably neither the youthful caddie nor the elderly professional is much given to any very minute analysis of the mental factors incident to golf. It is only he who takes up golf when well past his 'teens who finds that the motor centres have carefully to be taught and trained by the ideational centres; and probably not until the motor centres have learned to act largely by themselves does such golfer improve in his game. Probably, the more automatically one plays, the better one plays — which means that (unless one is a born athlete, or a muscular genius) one ought to commence golf very young indeed. (Zealous golfers had better enter their babies' names on the waiting lists of limited clubs.) For I take it that if the mind is strenuously occupied in trying to remember this, that, or the other particular rule for the stroke, some other rules are apt to be forgotten. That is to say, if the ideational or conceptual centres of the brain are too much occupied, some motor centres go disregarded. In the caddie and the professional probably at the moment of the stroke there is no ideation or conception going on whatsoever, the whole attention of the mind being in some incomprehensible way concentrated on the motor centres alone. All beginners — of a maturer age — find it impossible to remember — and obey — at every stroke all the rules they learn. — "What on earth," said one fair golfer to another once, "do you wear that ring on your thumb for?" — "To remind me of a certain rule." — "Good gracious!" said the other, "*I* should have to wear rings on my fingers and bells on my toes to remind me of all the rules I forget!"

Tale of ane fayre one.

I asked an admirable professional once, a man whose skill in tuition equalled his skill with the clubs, who thought out each stroke and excelled in the ætiology and diagnosis of the faults of his pupils, — I asked this professional to try to tell me precisely what it was that passed through his mind in that important but minute interval of time which elapsed between the raising of his club for the back-swing and its impact with the ball. He promised to do his best to find out, and his answer was as significant as it

A certaine authoritie interrogated.

was practical. "I canna find oot, Sorr," he said some days afterwards; "I dinna think I think aboot anything at a'. I juist luke at me ba'. Ef I do not luke at me ba', the stroke disna coom aff." Of an amateur to whom I put the same quæry, the reply was to the effect that if his mental attitude was at all reducible to verbal phraseology, it would probably take the form of the prayer of that Publican, who did not lift up so much as his eyes unto heaven, but smote upon his breast, saying, "God be merciful to me a sinner." *His replie.*

In one respect the professional and the caddie have an immense advantage over the amateur in golf: they are handling golf-clubs all day long; if they are not swinging them, they are making or mending them; they do nothing that tends to develope any set of muscles other than those brought into play in the game. And this is no unimportant point. The amateur rides or rows or *The professiounal and eke the cadet, they doe seem atte a vantage;*

shoots or yachts or fishes. Now, it may be a preposterous thing to assert, a thing that may arouse the derision of all but enthusiasts of the game, but it is highly probable that any form of exercise which brings into play and developes muscles not used in golf, or not used in the way that golf uses them, is injurious, not beneficial, to the golfer. If neither a violinist nor a pianist would dream of developing the muscles of his forearm and wrist by, say, hoeing or digging, neither should a golfer. I once knew a man who for a whole snowy winter did not touch a club, but daily visited a gymnasium and went through a variety of exercises for the express purpose of developing his muscles for his summer's golf—his ambition was long driving. What was the consequence? He confessed to me that that summer he was completely off his game! Another man I knew whose sole form of exercise that winter was walking and swinging golf clubs.

For that they do nought but playe.

This man's game improved vastly. The ex- *Sorrie*
planation probably lies in the fact that the *plights.*
nerve-currents by which the muscles are
contracted are very prone to run in the
tracks to which they are habituated; and if *Reasons pro-*
for several weeks or months they are made *pounded*
to travel in paths quite different from those *therefor.*
in which they must run—and swiftly and
accurately run—in the drive and the approach and the put, when they are ordered
to take the new direction they fail at first to
find it. No stoker or coal-heaver could suddenly become a card engraver; and if a
card engraver took to stoking or coal-heav-
ing, he would probably turn out very un-
saleable visiting-cards when first he re-
turned to his vocation. Everybody has
noticed how persistently the cricketing
stroke sticks to the cricketer who drops
cricket for golf in maturer years.—This
anatomical frame of ours is a wonderful
machine; we little know what slaves we are

to it. — The curious thing about golf is that adepts in all sorts of other and alien forms of sport think that there is no reason under heaven why they should not compel their anatomical frames to comply with the demands made upon them by the links. They excel, so they argue, in cricket or tennis racquets, why not in this ridiculously easy task of putting a ball into a hole? And when they fail, they become exasperated — and spend pounds in lessons — and pounds in implements of curious make — goose-necked putters, Schenectady putters, socket-headed drivers, aluminum cleeks — of these the name is Legion! There is not a game known to sportsmen in which failure so exasperates. Nay, it is not a game, if by "game" we mean a mere pass-time. Or, if it is, it is a method of passing the time than which few serious vocations so absorb the faculties, mental, moral, and, physical; or (shall we say?) so develope them. At least it is a game

Foolhardie ambitiouns.

in which earnestness, that moral attribute of character which seems now-a-days sometimes in serious danger of disparagement, in which earnestness ranks so high that, we may safely say, without it success is impossible.—I once heard of a lady champion who, in solitude, wept in sheer nervous tension over her victory. All honour to her tears!

Golfe, it is in treweth a praiseworthie pass-time.

X

However, after all this abstruse metaphysical and anatomical disquisition, shall we essay to discover practically what it is at bottom makes a man play well and what it is makes a man play ill; and what it is makes a man one day play well, and the next day ill? —Ah! he who could answer such quæries would tear the veil from Maia. Some men there be, of course, who will never play golf. Either they have a poor "eye"; or their mus-

Ye writer pauseth:

cular sense is but imperfectly developed; or
their keenness in sport is nil; or they are too
much taken up with the things of this world;
or they are men wrapt up in the contempla-
tion of so-called higher things. University
Inasmoche as professors I have known who, when they
golfe, it bin a ought to have had their eye upon the ball,
serious had their eye upon the clouds, and their
thynnge. minds farther off still. Other men I have
known to whom a round of golf was so casual and frivolous a pass-time that they
would seek to relieve the tædium of the
game (and perhaps entertain you!) by the
narration between strokes of interminable
and pointless anecdotes. Never by such men
will the Royal and Antient Game be properly played. By such men golf may be given
up at once and for ever. For maugre all ap-
pearances to the contrary, golf is one of the
most serious of sports. As well try to study
metaphysics indifferently, or to attack the
feminine heart indiscreetly, as try to play

[44]

golf listlessly. One cannot serve golf and
Mammon. Golf is the most jealous of mis- *Cautions.*
tresses. Are you worried and distrait; are
you in debt and expecting a dun; are stocks
unsteady and your margin small; is a note
falling due; or has a more than ordinarily
delicate feminine entanglement gone somewhat awry? Go not near the links. Take a
country walk, or go for a ride; drop into the
Club and ask numerous friends to assuage
their thirst; — do anything rather than attempt the simple task of putting a little ball
into a little hole. For to put that little ball
into that little hole — or rather into those
eighteen little holes — requires — requires
what? Alas! so many things, so many un- *Ye many*
thought-of-things. It requires, in the first *thynnges that*
place, a mind absolutely imperturbed, im- *be requisite.*
perturbable. You may play chess or bridge
or polo or poker on the eve of bankruptcy; I
defy you to play golf on the eve of a curtain
lecture. It takes a strong character to play

[45]

strong golf. Golf is as accurate an ethical criterion of a man as is the Decalogue. Perhaps this is why your rigid and Puritanical Scots Presbyterian plays so admirably. An eminent Scots philosopher once told me that the eminence of Scottish philosophy (note the Scottish appraisal of things Scottish, an you will) was due to the fact that Scots philosophers were brought up on the Shorter Catechism. I venture to think he might have extended his axiom to the St. Andrews game. — But, not to beat about the bush, this much is certain: golf is a game in which attitude of mind counts for incomparably more than mightiness of muscle. Given an equality of strength and skill, the victory in golf will be to him who is captain of his soul. Give me a clear eye, a healthy liver, a strong will, a collected mind, and a conscience void of offence both toward God and toward men, and I will back the pigmy against the giant. Golf is a test, not so much of the muscle, or even of the brain and nerves of a man, as it is a test of his inmost veriest self; of his soul and spirit; of his whole character and disposition; of his temperament; of his habit of mind; of the entire content of his mental and moral nature as handed down to him by unnumbered multitudes of ancestors. Does his pedigree date back to Romantic heroes — Frankish horsemen or Provençal Knights? Let him see to it that he curbs his impulsive Southern ardour. Does he trace his descent to the Vikings of the North, strenuous sea-kings that roamed afar and devasted foreign shores? Let him see to it that he applies himself to tasks more close at hand, that he wins him nearer victories. Is he a stolid Goth, bull-necked and big of loin? Let him see to it that the more agile-witted Kelt does not wrest victory from him by a deftness more delicate.

Howe thatte golfe yt tryeth ye inner manne.

Yet more cautions.

THE MYSTERY OF GOLF

XI

How to playe golfe well: BUT all this, again, is vague, theoretic, abstruse. What you, my confidential reader, seek, I know, is some simple, intelligible, practicable rule by which to determine how you, when you telegraph to an opponent and propose a match, shall be able to play transcendently well. What is it, precisely, that will enable you to go round under eighty to-day? — Confidential reader, did ever you hear tell of the elixir of life? Did ever you hear tell of the universal solvent? of the philosopher's stone? of the Sphinx her riddle? or of Fortunatus his cap? Mayhap you have. But mayhap you do not know that the secret of success in golf is more recondite, far more recondite, than is any one *'Tis a matere* of these. These be bagatelles compared *hard to come* with that. A greater fortune awaits him who *by:* will discover and divulge the mystery of golf than that which awaits him who will square the circle, explain the potentialities of radium, or solve the problem of the perpetuity of motion.—For, mark you, it is not against the fellow-man his human opponent that the golfer really wars. Nor is it even against Bogey that he pits his skill. The contest is with himself. There is no reason known amongst men why any golfer should ever get into a bunker. He knows, or he thinks he knows, exactly how every stroke in the round should be played. He may carry as many clubs as he likes, clubs of the most flagitious and flamboyant make. Most potent, grave, and reverend signors will stand stock-still and dumb the while he drives; and no thing on this terraqueous globe be permitted to impede his play. A sanguine flag gratuitously points out for him the hole; overtly printed on the sand-box or the score-card is the distance; his blameless ball (over the making of which countless rival manufacturers have expended an ingenuity

For nought impedeth the golfer; nay,

[49]

extreme) lies meekly at his feet—could Nature, or Art, or the Invention of Man farther go to expedite his way? It is Nature, it is Bogey, that are handicapped, not he;—and perchance it is the cognizance of the enormity of the responsibility thus laid upon him that appals the timorous golfer. The conditions are simple in the extreme: to knock a ball into a hole; and damp sand, and mown fields, and rolled greens, and caddie, and professional, and flag—to say nothing of cobbler's-wax, and rosin, and chalk, and hob-nails, and a red coat—contribute to aid him in coping with his foe.— Against whom do you contend if not against yourself?

Many thynnges do corage him.

Ah! But the conditions are the same for your opponent also. There's the rub. He too, therefore, wages a warfare against self. Accordingly golf resolves itself into this:— It is not a wrestle with Bogey; it is not a struggle with your mortal foe; it is a physio-

The golfer, his veritable foe—

logical, psychological, and moral fight with
yourself; it is a test of mastery over self; and *His owne*
the ultimate and irreducible element of the *selfe.*
game is to determine which of the players is
the more worthy combatant. You try to
prove to your opponent that you are a better man than he; and your opponent tries to
prove to you that he is a better man than
you; and the ordeal is decided by competition with a mutual and ideal foe, a foe mer-
ciless and implacable, a foe impeccable and
impartial, and that will by no means clear
the guilty. Golf is the refined modern equiv-
alent of the ancient barbarous Ordeal. To *Golfe—'tis*
support our claims to superiority to-day, we *an*
do not walk blind-fold and bare-foot over *ordeall:—*
nine red-hot plough-shares, we invite our
opponent to beat us in putting a ball into
eighteen holes; and we look to Pan—in the
shape of bunkers and hazards—to Defend
the Right;—and Pan is as inexorable as the
plough-shares.

[51]

XII

'Tis man against man. GOLF seems to bring the man, the very inmost man, into contact with the man, the very inmost man. In football and hockey you come into intimate — and often forcible enough — contact with the outer man; chess is a clash of intellects; but in golf character is laid bare to character. This is why so many friendships — and some enmities — are formed on the links. In spite of the ceremony with which the game is played: the elaborate etiquette, the punctilious adhesion to the honour, the enforced silence during the address, the rigid observance of rules, few if any games so strip a man of the conventional and the artificial. In a single round you can sum up a man, can say whether he be truthful, courageous, honest, upright, generous, sincere, slow to anger — or the reverse. — Of these arcana of golf the uninitiated onlooker knows

cious when found, as on the links. — To the Greeks this will be foolishness; to golfers a platitudinous truism.

For golf must be played "conscientiously" — so an eminent King's Counsel once remarked to me. He was right. The duffer imagines that at the very most it only requires a good "hand and eye" and some sort of knack. A good eye and a very large amount of skill it certainly does need; but he who thinks that these are the Alpha and Omega of golf will be apt to remain a duffer long. Between this Alpha and this Omega is a whole alphabet. Golf requires the most concentrated mental attention. It requires also just as concentrated a moral attention. The moral factors in the game are as important as the physical. He who succumbs to temptation will have to succumb to defeat. *Satis imperat,* says an old *The writer* adage, *qui sibi est imperiosus:* he rules enough *citeth.* who rules himself. This should be the motto of every golfer. "If one man conquer in a battle a thousand times a thousand men," says the Dhammapada with oriental extravagance, "and if another conquer himself, he is the greatest of conquerors," a text which is brought home to one in every round. "Greater," said Solomon, "is he that ruleth himself than he that taketh a city." In golf the ruler of himself will take many a hole. —And in truth the golfer knows this, and many and curious sometimes are the means he adopts to attain this end. Every reader will recall the idiosyncrasies of his friends, even if he cannot recall his own: how one will regale himself on stout and steak, and another lunch off chicken and tea; how Robinson will order a tankard of ale, and Anderson a tumbler of Scotch; how Bibulus will challenge Asceticus to take another helping of pie, and Asceticus respond by challenging Bibulus to wash it down with liqueur; how Fumosus will smoke cigars or

Extraneous and eke adventitious aides,

By the which to overcome certaine difficulties.

cigarettes the whole round through, and Abstemius resolutely leave his pipe in his locker; how Medicus will seek by diet or drugs to eliminate this or that unheard-of acid from his frame, and Hereticus live high to accomplish the same purpose. — The cellar and the pantry of a Golf Club, an they would, could divulge many a tale. And all, what for? To "bring under," as Saint Paul saith, this pervicacious body of ours, or to brace this puny soul of ours to the conflict so that we shall not "beat the air," as saith Saint Paul again.

XIV

THE thousand and one things that we should *not* do in golf are evidence of the difficulties of the game. In no other game must immense strength go hand in hand with extreme delicacy. If a fraction of a square inch of wood or steel does not come in contact with a fraction of a cubic inch of

These described.

[57]

gutta-percha exactly *so* and not otherwise, you are landed in a bunker, or you fly off to one side, or you over-run the hole. And in every stroke in golf this nicety of accuracy is necessary. If in the Drive the whole weight and strength of the body, from the nape of the neck to the soles of the feet, are not transferred from body to ball through the minute and momentary contact of club with ball absolutely surely, yet swiftly — you top, or you pull, or you sclaff, or you slice, or you swear (let us hope episcopally: which, being interpreted, according to the annecdote, signifieth silently). So with the Put. Not even an expert dare be careless of his stance or his stroke even for the shortest of Puts. And as to that Mashie shot, where you loft high over an abominable bunker and fall dead with a back spin and a cut to the right on a keen and declivitous green — is there any stroke in any game quite so delightfully difficult as that?

Analysis of the Drive

Not only is the stroke in golf an extremely difficult one, it is also an extremely
complicated one, more especially the Drive,
in which its principles are accentuated. It is
in fact a subtile combination of a swing and
a hit; the "hit" portion being deftly incorporated into the "swing" portion just as the
head of the club reaches the ball, yet without disturbing the regular rhythm of the
motion. The whole body must turn on the *Anatomicall*
pivot of the head of the right thigh-bone *explanatioun*
working in the cotyloidal cavity of the *os in-* *of the stroke*
nominatum or nameless bone, the head, right *atte golfe.*
knee, and right foot remaining fixed, with
the eyes riveted on the ball. In the upward
swing, the vertebral column rotates upon
the head of the right femur, the right knee
being fixed; but as the club-head nears the
ball, the fulcrum is rapidly changed from
the right to the left hip, the spine now rotat-
ing on the left thigh-bone, the left knee
being fixed; and the velocity is accelerated

by the arms and wrists, in order to add the force of the muscles to the weight of the body, thus gaining the greatest impetus possible. Not every professional instructor has succeeded in putting before his pupil this anatomical exposition of the correct stroke in golf. "Juist swoop her awa', maister," says one instructor. "*Hit* ut, mon," says another. Both are right, but such apparently discordant admonitions puzzle the neophyte. The professional also never wearies of telling you to "follow through"— the phrase has become almost a bye-word and a hissing on the links. But the "follow through" is merely evidence of three things: that you have poised the body properly; that you have swung correctly; and that you have "hit" at the moment of impact without destroying the rhythm; though probably the endeavour to "follow through" is an aid towards the correct accomplishment of these three things. The complexity of this movement is,

Ye "followe thorough," what it signifieth.

Analysis of the Drive

I take it, one of the chiefest of the difficulties in golf, and the one hardest to be surmounted by the unyouthful novice. No stroke in any other game is quite like it; so that proficiency in other games is neither a criterion of, nor a preparation for, proficiency in golf.

One comfortable thing there is about golf: it does not need any excessive training. You need not reduce your weight, as you must for steeple-chasing; you need not be desperately careful about your wind, as you must be if you are entering for the half-mile or the mile. The heavy-weight and the light-weight are evenly matched on the links. Indeed an illustrious exponent of the game has said in print that it is as well that the golfer should pursue his ordinary mode of living, that he should make no extraordinary variation from his regular regimen. If he is accustomed to his pipe and his glass, well and good. So far so good. But there is

Certaine consideratiouns comfortynge to the blythesome golfer.

this to be said. Golf above all things needs the steadiest of nerves, the clearest eye, and

And yette—
how
exactinge
golfe it be:

the most imperturbable of brains. If you are given to burning the midnight oil over books—or bridge, the odds will be against you on the links. Perhaps, as a matter of fact, golf is more exacting than a steeple-chase or the half-mile: it tries endurance; it tries the judgment; it tries the temper. No kind of sport sooner finds out a man's weak point than does golf. Two or three months will put you in trim for polo; golf demands the training of a lifetime. In golf this hu-

Alack!

man machine of ours is put to the sever-est test; and if it has been overworked or abused, it is more than likely to break down between the teeing-ground and the green.

XV

YET not a little has been said, in a semi-sar-castic way, by devotees of other games than golf, about the comparative ease with which

—as the sayers aver—a stationary ball can *Refutatioun* be, or should be, struck, as compared with *of ye dis-* one in motion. These detractors forget the *prizement of* nicety of the stroke that is required. A ten- *difficultie.* nis-player has a whole court into which to play; a cricketer a whole field; the golfer has to put his ball into a hole of the size of a jam-pot, a quarter of a mile away. Indeed, the difficulties of golf are innumerable and *The chiefest* incalculable. Take, for example, that simple *of the reules* rule, "Keep your eye on the ball." It is un- *of golfe:* heard of in tennis; it is needless in cricket; in golf it is iterated and reiterated times without number—and infringed as often as repeated. Yet not everybody, I think, knows the reasons of the tendency to infringe it. One of them is this: As anatomists know, the crystalline lens in the eye automatically accommodates itself, by means of the cil- iary muscle, to the focus of the object looked at. Now, many players get into the habit of looking intently at the flag, then

suddenly reverting their gaze to their ball
and striking before the lens has adapted itself to the new and nearer focus, with the
result that they see the ball indistinctly and
hit inaccurately. It is not that one does not
look at one's ball; it is that one does not take
time to look properly. To prove my theory,
let anyone gaze steadfastly at a distant object and then quickly direct the eye to one
close at one's foot. To learn that it requires
time for the outlines of the latter to grow
definite and distinct will be a lesson he will
find invaluable on the links.

How that it
bin lesse
simple
thanne to the
unthinking it
seemeth.

But indeed upon this all-important and
fundamental rule, "Keep your eye on the
ball," there might be written, by him who
had ability for the task, a whole Baconian
essay, for in this rule is comprised all the law
and the prophets. In itself this injunction
seems simplicity itself; to the practical carrying out thereof there are obstacles insupera-
ble. I have touched on the difficulties inci-

dent to the focussing of the crystalline lens; yet these, compared with obstacles less obvious, are nearly negligible—at least to youth. To youth the focussing of the crystalline lens is happily not only automatic, but instantaneous; 'tis age has to be patient and circumspect—in golf as in all things else: youth cuts the Gordian knot; age, poor age, saws through it.—But I digress. One of the chiefest impediments to a rigid observance of this the chiefest of rules lies in the fact that almost always the unpracticed golfer has an incontinent desire to see whither his ball is going before even he has hit it. The desire may be natural, but, without the shadow of a doubt, to indulge it is fatal. James Braid in his "How to Play Golf" has found for this desire an ingenious explanation. "The fact seems to be," he says, "that the mind, and the optic nerve through it, works rather more quickly than the arms and the body." It may be so. This

Ane explicatioun propounded.

mind of man is a highly culpable entity, and the optic nerve should have more sense than to yield to its demands. Men have I known, not a few, who resort to adventitious aids by which to thwart its nefarious designs. Only last week a golfer of repute, in the smoking-room of my club, frankly avowed that he took a caddie, not so much for the purpose of carrying his clubs, as because, when he had a caddie, he was less apt to take his eye *Moralizings* off his ball. — How peccant, how very pec- *thereuponne.* cant, human nature is! The mind of man, so it seems, even when most intent on the most important business in hand, is so indisciplinable, so incorrigible, so ungovernable by the owner of that mind himself, that that owner has perforce artificially to avoid a temptation which he feels he cannot resist.

Again, curiously enough, if you impress upon yourself too anxiously this maxim calling upon you to look at your ball, you will find yourself deprived of the power to look at it at all, as a man who tries to count *And, alack-* his own pulse unconsciously perturbs it. *a-daye, how* Your eye wanders back and forth; you look *hedged* at the top of the abiding sphere; you look at *abouten with* its back; often you look at your club instead *unknowne* of at your ball. As a matter of fact, instead *foemen.* of *looking,* you are *thinking;* and to *think,* when you ought to *play,* is the madness of mania.

"What then," so do I imagine an irasci- *Certaine* ble reader to ejaculate, "what then the use *warnynges.* of all this learned descant on the Mystery of Golf, and all these numerous attempts by tutors and writers to elucidate for me the intricacies and complexities of this abominable game, if I may not on the links think upon and carry out their lucubrations?"— I prithee give us grace. Theorize not when you are playing in a match. Theorize in your study, experiment when you practise; but if you do not wish to go forth to certain defeat—and of a surety to the taking of your eye off your ball, cease you from theorizing in a match. For, to think out a stroke implies diffidence in that stroke; and than diffidence there is not a more fatal foe to golf.

The summe of ye matere.

Howsoever, to sum up: until a man his learned to keep his eye on his ball, he will not play golf. He may be an excellent fellow; he may be the most jovial of companions, the sagest of counsellors, and the truest of friends; but unless he can keep his eye on his ball, never will he be a golfer.

Golfe & charactere.

Indeed, sometimes I am inclined to think that for a man invariably to be able to keep this one commandment, he must be *good;* that perhaps only the man who could keep the ten commandments could keep this one. For, mark you, it requires so many virtues, certainly that greatest of Tennyson his trinity, self-control. Not every good man will be a good golfer; but I challenge any one to dispute the fact that every really good golfer will at heart be a good man. Golf, in short, is not so much a game as it is a creed and a religion. Only the man who has not learned how thoroughly under control he must keep his mind, his body, and his morals, will dispute that assertion. —

I have said that art and sport are near akin. Are not art and sport and religion very nearly akin?

Perchaunce an audacious sayinge.

Besides, not every one knows the full significance of that simple verb "to look" in this simple but cardinal injunction. You must "look" with the most concentrated and absorbed attention. A casual or half-hearted look is suicidal. And you must look with the mind's eye as well as with the sensory one—and the one must be as keen, as clear, and as alert as the other.

To "looke," what in treueth it meaneth.

XVI

THE difficulties of golf are immense. For think for a moment: there is scarcely a muscle in the body that is not called into play;

Difficulties ensampled,

and every muscle is controlled by a nerve. In fact, every muscle is a bundle of fibres or spindles, and every fibre or spindle is controlled by a branch of a nerve, cannot contract save in response to a stimulus conveyed to it by a branch of a nerve. Unless an order is sent from the brain and distributed to each and every part of the machinery which moves the trunk and limbs, not a movement can be made. And to ensure harmonious and coördinate movement, those orders must be very carefully, not only *And* timed, but apportioned. Indeed, it would *comments* seem that duplicate orders, that two sets of *thereon.* stimuli, have to be despatched. There is, first, that which governs the "muscular sense," or, as some physiologists prefer to call it, the kinæsthesis, the sense that determines how tightly to hold the club and that poises the body for the swing. It is the sense, speaking generally, which ensures the proper relative rigidity or flexibility of opposing flexor and extensor muscles. It is chiefly concerned in judging distance, and is especially noticeable in the short Approach. In the second place, there is the hit or swing. This is the office of the motor centres, and is brought about by a strong contraction of muscles, a contraction that should be rapidly yet perfectly evenly increased. Both sets of stimuli must be intimately and intricately combined throughout the whole course of the swing: the wrists must ease off at the top and tauten at the end; the left knee must be loose at the beginning and firm at the finish; and the change from one to the other must be as deftly and gently, yet swiftly wrought, as a crescendo passage from pianissimo to fortissimo on a fiddle.

Explicatiouns, it maye be, somewhat recondite.

XVII

Is it possible, from this physiological point of view, to determine what is the funda-

An inquirie concerning what it bin tendeth to make a golfer to excell.

mental difference between a good player and a bad? Can we say what it is makes a great golfer? At first sight one is inclined to answer, As well try to find out what makes a great general, a great poet, or a great artist. Genius plays as large a part on the links as it does in life; and "genius," the dictionary says, "implies the possession of high and peculiar natural gifts which enable their possessor to reach his ends by a sort of intuitive power." However, leaving the genius out of view as beyond the reach of ordinary explanation, what is it that enables one man always to go round under eighty and another

Of mimicrie. never? Well, for one thing, I suspect Imitation plays a large part in golf—as indeed it does in all life. Dr. Alfred Russel Wallace and Professor Poulton have pointed out its importance in biology, and Professor Yrjö Hirn its importance in art. Mimicry it is, probably—whatever in its ultimate analysis mimicry may be—which is at the bottom of all education; that by which we learn to talk no less than to golf. The youthful caddie probably picks up the game by sheer unconscious imitation, and his motor centres being highly docile, the correct golfing swing comes to him with ease — as a child learns to talk simply by hearing its parents. The man who takes up golf at thirty or forty, when the motor centres are by no means docile, and the nerve currents have been for years accustomed to flow in very different channels, — cricket channels and tennis channels, — the elderly beginner has to learn golf as a man learns a new language, by accidence and prosody. If he can imitate his professional, well and good, but he will in all probability have also to apply himself assiduously to the grammar of the game. But to imitate requires the innervation of nerve centres in the brain — all unconscious, or rather all sub-conscious, as no doubt that innervation is.

In olden age one learneth ye game as one learneth grammaire.

*An anatomi-
call disquisi-
tioun.*

To begin at the bottom then, if the physiologists are not all wrong, to excel in golf requires first of all a good brain. There is a
part of the brain called the corpora striata.
"The corpora striata," say the neurologists,
"are great motor ganglia in some way concerned with the execution of voluntary,
emotional, and ideo-motor movements."[*]
"The Corpus Striatum," says Broadbent,
"...translates volitions into actions, or puts
in execution the commands of the intellect;
that is, it selects, so to speak, the motor
nerve nuclei in the medulla and cord appropriate for the performance of the desired
action, and sends down the impulses which
set them in motion."[†] Nor is that all. In
co-operation with the corpora striata is
the cerebellum, which "co-ordinates move-

[*]*The Brain as an Organ of Mind.* By H. Charlton
Bastian, London, 1880, p. 564.
[†]*British Medical Journal,* April 1, 1876. Quoted by
Bastian, *op. cit.,* p. 567.

ments...or combines the general movements...ordered by volition" *(Ib.)*. — That is to say, if you want to move your arms and legs together *so*, you must call upon the striate bodies and the little brain to convey the orders; and if the *so* is a highly complicated and delicate series of movements, they must be good striate bodies and a good little brain to be equal to it; and to these undoubtedly we must add a good medulla and a good spinal cord to boot.

Secondly, given a first-class corpus striatum and a cerebellum equally good, these two parts of the brain, together with the cord and all the nerve-cells and fibres by which they operate, must be educated, by constant practice, to perform smoothly, quickly, and forcibly the complex motions necessary for the peculiar stroke of golf. This, I take it, is done by what Professor Loeb calls the "associative memory." The associative memory is a very important af-

The "associative memorie," what yt ben.

[75]

fair indeed. Loeb goes so far as to make it synonymous with the will, with self-consciousness, with the Ego! Yet its office and function are simple, namely to ensure the almost automatic sequence of such movements as have previously been deliberately and hesitatingly combined. The golf stroke is a highly complex one, and one necessitating the innervation of innumerable cerebro-spinal centres. Not only hand and eye, but arm, wrist, shoulders, back, loins, and legs must be stimulated to action. No wonder that the associative memory has to be most carefully cultivated in golf. To be able, without thinking about it, to take your stance, do your waggle, swing back, pause, come forward, hit hard, and follow through well over the left shoulder, always self-confidently—ah! this requires a first-class brain, a first-class spinal cord, and first-class muscles.

What the anatomists say is this, that, if

the proper orders are issued from the cortex, and gathered up and distributed by the corpora striata and the cerebellum, are then transferred through the crus cerebri, the pons varolii, and the anterior pyramid of the medulla oblongata, down the lateral columns of the spinal cord into the anterior cornua of grey matter in the cervical, the dorsal, and the lumbar region, they will then "traverse the motor nerves at the rate of about a hundred and eleven feet a second and speedily excite definite groups of muscles in definite ways with the effect of producing the desired movements" (Bastian).

The anatomiste, his tale:

"Definite ways" and "desired movements" "speedily excited"! Gramercy! Are not these THE *desiderata* in golf?

The futilitie thereof.

But Bastian and Broadbent, I shall be told, are a bit out of date. Let me then quote Sherrington, a pre-eminent neurologist of the day.—Sherrington has tried to

An exposition more near to hande.

find out what it is that determines the final and definite movement of a set of muscles when more than one stimulus exists. His experiments were made on a dog. Would they had been made on a golfer, for if any one thing is patent to the indifferent golfer it is that he has to attend to a terrible lot of stimuli; and to which particular stimulus his muscles will respond he would give a great deal to know. (What duffer can tell beforehand whether he is going to slice or to pull, to baff or to top?) Sherrington, after a series of careful investigations argues thus: "The motor paths at any moment accord in a united pattern for harmonious synergy, coöperating for one effect.... The struggle between dissimilar arcs for mastery over their final common path takes place in the synaptic field at origin of the final neurones. ... The issue of that conflict—namely, the determination of which competing arc shall for the time being reign over the final com-

Messer Sherrington, how he interpreteth certaine subtile thynnges.

mon path—is largely conditioned by three factors. One of these is the relative intensity of the stimulation.... A second main determinant.... is the functional species of those reflexes.... A third main factor deciding the conflict between the competing reflexes is 'fatigue.'... The animal mechanism is thus given solidarity by this principle which for each effector organ allows and regulates interchange of the arcs playing upon it, a principle which I would briefly term that of 'the interaction of reflexes about their common path.'"* That is to say, muscles are *His interpre-* moved by orders issued by the neurone or *tatioun inter-* nerve centre governing those muscles; when *preted.* this neurone receives conflicting orders from headquarters, it transmits only one, and this one is determined by *(a)* its strength; *(b)* its character; or *(c)* its freshness. Accordingly, the task for the golfer is by no

Address to the Physiological Section of the British Association for the Advancement of Science, 1904.

means an easy one, for he has to move several sets of muscles, and he has to see to it
that the orders issued to their respective
neurones are strong, are of a particular
The practicall character, and are fresh. If he does not know
worthe what sort of an order to issue: if, for in-
thereof. stance, he forgets for the fractional part of a
second, any one of the numerous injunc-
tions imperative for a proper stroke—the
firm grip, the eye on the ball, the head
steady, the right foot fixed, the rhythmic
back-swing, the twirl of the wrists, the accelerated velocity, the hit at the impact, the glo-
rious follow-through, to say nothing of the
preliminary stance, waggle, judging of distance, and correct angle of feet, elbows,
body, and what-not—well, all I can say is
that woe betides him. "The multiplicity of
the conflict," says Sherrington, "seems extreme." We can positively assure him that
it is.

I am afraid, however, that unless these

learned anatomists and neurologists can *All thys* also tell us some remedy for improperly is- *profiteth not* sued and incorrectly communicated orders, *him who* I am afraid their lucubrations will be of no *playeth ill.* very great practical value to the golfer who is off his game. It would be a comfort to find out what portion of the anatomical apparatus really was at fault. It would be a comfort to be able to fix the blame, say, on the infundibulum of the pituitary body or the valve of Vieussens. Which the offending centre is, I am afraid we shall not know till some foozling golfer submits to trepanning. —Perhaps not even then; for if, as I believe is the case, no alienist has yet been able to discover a cerebral lesion in the lunatic, it is not likely that the surgeon will find one in the foozler.

And yet it is always some unknown but sinning centre that the erring golfer blames. The bad workman used to complain of his tools; but, with numberless tools to choose

*How that
the golfer, he
resorteth to
subterfuge—
even as did
Adam.*

from, and with absolute power of choice, the bad golfer is perforce driven to complain of some part of himself.—Never himself apparently.—The Old Adam dies hard. It is always one's digestion, or one's liver, or one's suprarenal capsules that are at fault.—Which is a curious ethico-psychological fact.—At all events it is a tremendous compliment to the fascination of golf that it is to these technical adumbrations of the anatomist that we are driven in order to explain or to excuse the vagaries of our game. One does not get "off" one's football in this way, or one's chess or one's poker or one's bridge; and if one did, one would hardly go to neurology or to histological pathology for the cause.

XVIII

*Quærie: Who
accuseth
whom?*

AND yet, what, after all, do these innumerable excuses that the poor golfer invents for himself after a bad round mean? Whom or what is he blaming? Is he not made up of cerebral and cerebellar centres; of cranial and spinal nerves; of neurones and synaptic fields; of extensor and flexor muscles? Are they not *he?* Which is the blamer and which is the blamed? Is there some inscrutable and immaterial psychic centre, inerrant and supreme, that sits enthroned aloft, and sways and rules these lesser centres? Shall we find in golf proof of the existence of a Soul?

Of a soul! If the physical mysteries of golf are so recondite, what of the psychic? These, I fear, be beyond us. How analyse the complexities of the human golfing soul? How tread the labyrinthine mazes of temperament and of character? How unravel the mesh-work of feelings and emotions, hopes and desires and fears, exultations and disappointments, heated angers, heavy despondencies; the wrath so hard to allay or ere the sun goes down; the vain imaginings, the ridiculous puffings-up of our little souls, of our silly little souls, over a hole halved in three or a circumvented stymie? Or how explain the disturbances these bring about in the higher layers, and the resulting delinquencies of the motor muscles?—In golf we see in its profoundest aspect that profound problem of the relation of mind to matter. Nowhere in the sum-total of the activities of life is this puzzle presented to us in acuter shape than on the links. Is there an ideal and immaterial Self in the golfer which knows precisely what it wants to do; and a bodily and fleshly one that will not or cannot carry out its behests? Is there an immaterial mind, superior to, but linked with, a material brain; or does the brain, in its subtlest interstices, shade off into an immaterial mind—a thing unimaginable by man? Does matter *think?* Are beef and mutton and cabbage and potatoes transmuted into mind?—

Golfe doth provide matere for meditation.

[84]

Mind and Matter

We misuse words. We construct an artificial and needless barrier between mind and matter. By "matter" we simply mean something perceptible by our five senses; and by "mind" we simply mean something imperceptible by these senses. What "matter" really is we know as little as we do what "mind" really is. Suppose we had fifty senses; suppose we could actually perceive electricity, magnetism, æthereal vibrations, molecular motion, radial emanations, the interplay of emotion, the working of memory, the miracle of thought; suppose we could detect every and all of the myriad manifestations of energy as exhibited in the whole of this wonderful world! Would not the barrier be very hastily thrown down, and matter reveal itself as in reality one and the same with mind?

Whether minde and matere, they be not identicall.

How extraordinarily limited is our conception of matter — so we call it! We say it has weight, colour, shape, sound, smell, tex-

Of matere.

[85]

ture, temperature, or taste—just seven or eight properties, just seven or eight (for "energy" is but a name for the unknown)! And every one of these is highly problematical, and even vanishes altogether under certain conditions: there is no weight at the centre of the earth; form and colour disappear in the dark; and all the rest go with paralysis or *Speculatiouns* paresis. What if matter had six or seven *abstruse, and* hundred properties? What if mind had an *it maye be,* infinite number of senses—or rather, what *sillie.* if mind required no senses for the perception of matter? Would not percipient mind and perceptible matter prove themselves identical; and perhaps the soul of man find itself coincident and conterminous with the Soul of the universe?

XIX

SPECULATIONS such as these carry us far. I seem to see in the conscientious golfer, doing his utmost, poor soul, to make matter

(or mind) transcend its own powers, a type and symbol of mankind; of mankind warring with its environment, striving to overcome its limitations, reaching up to some unknown ideal, pressing towards some inscrutable goal.—What potentialities may not lurk in Man! If Amœba has developed into Man, into what may not Man develope! Some day we shall get some arch-angelical record rounds.—I wonder what Par Golf on the New Jerusalem links will be!—But these be transcendental themes.

The golfer, an epitome of man, his kinde;

One more speculative point, and we will drop metaphysics.—The golfer, strive as he may, is the slave of himself. Perhaps nothing is borne in upon the golfer more strongly after months of practice than that his place on the Club Handicap is determined by this his slavery to himself. There is not a golfer living but would say, "If I could, I would." The links prove the fatal and irrefragable chain of cause and effect. Every golfer *wills*

And eke a slave unto himselfe.

to excel, and every golfer sedulously searches for the causes of failure. — 'Tis only one more proof of the transcendental identity of mind and matter. If, as the biologists aver, *omnis cellula e cellulâ,* and ratiocination and emotion are impossible without cells, surely then also *omnis idea ex ideâ,* and thought and volition are links in an interminable chain....

XX

Whether or not ther be underselven.

THE net-work of chains in the golfer's brain must be multitudinous. Golf seems to afford a corroboration of the theory that there are in man several layers of consciousness. Indeed, the late Mr. F. W. H. Myers might have found in golf a pertinent proof of the existence of his "subliminal self," to the functions of which he attributed so important a share. Why a man should, say in June, play a superlatively excellent game, and in July play an execrable one, in spite of the

fact that he is in July just as fit as he was in June, that passes the wit of that man, poor wight! He broods over it; he almost weeps over it; he tries remedy after remedy, but in vain—beef and beer, total abstinence; a more elaborate waggle, no waggle; right foot forward, left foot firmer; a cigar before a game, no tobacco at all—all to no purpose. He knows to a nicety how every stroke should be played; but he is blessed, so he says, if he can play it. — Can it be that the so-called human "individual" is after all a duple, triple, quadruple, quintuple, or multiple personality? Almost it would seem so. *So, in fay, it* You take your stance at the first tee, and *seemeth.* Personality No. I severely makes up his mind to play carefully and well. At the approach, Personality No. II presses. At the put, Personality No. III is over-anxious, and is short. At the second tee, Personality No. IV flings care to the four winds of heaven. No. V takes his eye off the ball. No. VI goes into a bunker. No. *n* swears (let us hope subliminally). By this time the exasperated golfer compares himself to the Gadarene demoniac.

How golfe, it appeareth to possess an influence trewely fiendlich;

Indeed, a veritable demon seems to enter into a man on the links. Otherwise what on earth possesses him that he should transgress the most elementary and the most easily obeyed of rules? Why should he take his eye off his ball? Why should he "press" or hurry his stroke? There lies his ball awaiting his pleasure, and would await it for a fortnight, for that matter— there is not even a time-limit for the address; and every spectator, by the stern etiquette of the game, is in duty bound to stand mute and patient the while he prepares to strike. What on earth possesses him that he should look up before he strikes or strike in a hurry? And yet man after man spoils stroke upon stroke by these infantine follies—and, worse and worse, spoils them consecutively! There is no phys-

ical or artificial impediment whatsoever.
Some ninety or a hundred yards of level
turf lie between ball and hole. A club precisely made to suit that particular shot is
handed you. Time and time again you have
been taught exactly how to stand, exactly
how to swing. And yet how often it has
taken three, four, and even five strokes to
cover those hundred yards! It would be *And*
laughable were it not so humiliating. In fact *doth move*
the impudent spectator does laugh — until *derisioun.*
he tries it himself; then, ah! then, he too gets
a glimpse into that miracle of miracles, the
human mind, which at one and the same
time wills to do a thing and fails to do it;
which knows precisely and could repeat by
rote the exact means by which it is to be accomplished, yet is impotent to put them in
force. And the means are so simple, so in-
sanely simple. We need not be surprised
that the impudent spectator does not even
affect to conceal his laughter in his sleeve.

—But neither need we be surprised that the experts, the adepts, those who have gone through the humiliation of failure, watching these puerilities from the veranda, are moved rather to wonder than to laughter. They have had more glimpses into the profundities and complexities of the erring golfing mind than they care to reckon, and they know that the secret of this extraordinary and baffling conflict of mind and matter is a psychological problem beyond the reach of physiology and ontology combined.

Yette not in hem that have suffered tribulatioun.

XXI

The golfer his minde likened unto a citie ful of folke;

TALK as neurologists and psychologists may, what this fearfully and wonderfully made thing called "mind" is we have not the remotest conception. *Five* layers of consciousness? Why, there is a whole civic community underneath each one of us his hat or her bonnet. Trained watchmen sit at eye-gate and ear-gate and touch-gate and smell-gate and taste-gate, and report to the Mayor and Aldermen of Mansoul regarding all personages who demand admission. Go on board ship, and not until the watchmen have assured themselves that the sound and vibration of the screw are harmless, will they let the city sleep, though the central council argue never so hard. Let the screw stop at the end of the voyage, and immediately the watchmen rouse the whole city, shouting that something has gone wrong. And, if the encephalon is a municipality, the bodily frame is, as it were, a whole nation under its government, whence, according to reports received from the portals, orders are issued for the mobilization of forces and the undertaking of huge campaigns—one battalion of muscles holding the legs in firm position; another sending the arms flying in all directions. And—

And eke his bodie like unto a nation.

mystery of mysteries, miracle among things miraculous — not only are there guards and officials and troops, but apparently there is a Generalissimo or an Emperor, who can look on and analyse and criticise the doings and functions of this nation and capital — can actually try to discover the method of its own working and put down in black and white the provisions of its own constitution; for surely, reader, this is precisely what you and I are attempting to do at this moment! The mind itself, so it seems, can turn round upon itself, get outside of itself, and examine its own workings! What a stupendous puzzle! Ah! there must be more in the human mind than watchmen and aldermen and mayor; there must be lords spiritual as well as temporal — perhaps a shrine and *Speculatiouns* altar, and, behind a veil, a Holy of Holies. *Neo-* In microcosmic Mind I seem to see in *Platonique.* miniature a tiny facsimile or homologue of macrocosmic Spirit, that Spirit which not only externalizes itself in Nature, but, as Plotinus of Lycopolis hath it, "possesses sight and knowledge of itself" (*apud* Tennemann).

But alas! how often the little microcosm goes wrong! How desperately ignorant it is of itself!—Well, few things bring home to us better the depths of this our ignorance of ourselves than its vagaries and eccentricities on the links. What particular giant-cell in the cortex of the brain fails to act when we take our eye off our ball? Will any electrode teach us that? And what cortical monitor indignantly upbraids that cell immediately afterwards? Will any theory of "multiple personality" explain for us that? Constantly one part of the mind takes another to task for dereliction of duty. Cannot the mind see *Golfe, an* to it that the municipality as a whole and *inner* the nation under its rule act in unison? Can *combatte,* it be that there is going on in each individual human being a gigantic constitutional

[95]

struggle exactly analogous to that which is going on and has ever been going on in every nation upon this terrene periphery—a struggle to determine who shall rule, what powers the ruler shall have, and how his actions may be checked? So it would seem.—

Looked at nearly, golf does, indeed, raise for our consideration deep and curious questions. But golf cannot answer them, any more than can the neurologists or the psychologists—or, for the matter of that, the constitutional historians. For in golf, so it would appear, the political constitution of this little human individual community is put to the severest and utmost test. So extremely complex, requiring the harmonious coöperation of so many sets of forces, is the task imposed by golf, that the whole body politic is thrown, every time it sets out on a round, into the throes of a constitutional crisis. A huge and difficult political problem suddenly confronts it, a problem for the cor-

Whilk instituteth a search for ane to guide.

rect solution of which the nation must act harmoniously and as a unit. The Republic is in danger, and the inhabitants rush about looking for one whom to appoint as Dictator. — *Or*, as the French say, well for that man among whose myriad cell-population there is always a Cincinnatus ready to leave his plough and *attend to the game!* for unless there is, there will be consternation in the capital, and no concerted action, but only vague hurryings and recriminations, and rushings to and fro of disorderly mobs. But alas! Cincinnati are rare, very, very rare. It takes a great national cataclysm to throw up a great leader of men. Only, indeed, in *Of* great cataclysms are great men thrown up. *cataclysmes.* What an upheaval produced a Napoleon, what a revolution a Washington! Ordinary events do not produce extraordinary men. —Perhaps this is why an extraordinary round can be performed only by an extraordinary player.

The unseemlie lack of rationalitie that ther be in golfe.

What exasperates the ordinary man about golf is that it seems to be a game utterly and absolutely unamenable to reason. You may speculate in stocks; you may lay odds on a horse-race; but the money-market and the turf are child's play compared with the uncertainties of golf;—and this in spite of the fact that, though you cannot control the market, and know your horse only by hearsay, on the links it is on your own individual efforts that you count. My opponent to-day had had a bad night; so he dolefully told me, and expected defeat. What was the result? His record round for his links!—No; golf is not amenable to reason.—And here we find another factor in the extraordinary fascination of the game.

An adage.

—The unknown, says Tacitus, is always the wondered at. Well, metaphysics, golf, and the feminine heart will be wondered at long. —But from a search for the causes of the uniqueness of golf, we have been led into

taken up golf before you proposed," said a
wife once.—It is related, too, of a famous
Anglican Divine—a Doctor of Divinity *A chesteine-*
(and I think this story is not quite a chest- *nutte—most*
nut)—that, having come under the spell of *like.*
the sport, in a burst of unecclesiastical
frankness he confided to a friend that there
was that in the game which made him forget his wife, his family, his country, and his
God.

XXIII

Is this uniqueness explicable? Well, per- *Wherein*
haps in no other game, for one thing, are *lieth this*
you obliged, or have you time, so intensely *uniquenesse*
to concentrate your every faculty on your
every stroke. In no other game have you
so to be master of yourself, as it were,
to steady yourself,—your muscles, your
nerves, your brain, nay, your mood, and
your temper,—or to be master of yourself

for so long a stretch. Four or five score strokes must be made, some of them with the strength of a sledge-hammer, many of them with the delicacy of a microtome, all of them with the precision of a machine; and so to subdue this unruly body of ours, with its mobile muscles, its ebullient blood, its unquiet nerves, its perturbable brain, as to achieve that feat...one has to pass through much tribulation or ere that feat is even approximately achieved. In no other game are you left so desperately alone. In no other game does all depend upon your individual effort. There is nothing to hamper you, nothing to hinder you, nothing to hurry you.

The precisioun nedeful atte golfe.

Golf is so deliberate that the mind has ample time in which to act—another feature which differentiates it from other sports. In fact, the difference between a rapid game like tennis and a deliberate game like golf is similar to the difference between playing a piece of music with *Peculiarities* which you are familiar and reading note by *of golfe.* note a piece of music that is new. In the one the fingers move spontaneously; in the other they are guided at every step by the brain. In no game, too, does so much depend upon a single stroke. In a three-days' cricket match tens of thousands of hits must be made; in three sets out of five in tennis certainly tens of hundreds; in the most important of matches in golf never so many as a couple of hundred; the intrinsic and proportionate importance of each hit being thus correspondingly increased. Nor in any other game are the conditions so *Compari-* fixed and invariable. In tennis, cricket, polo, *souns put* racquets, the conditions change momentar- *y-forthe.* ily; before you have time to think, you have to strike at a ball coming at a different angle and with a different velocity and with a different cut from those of the one before; and you must strike it with a corresponding difference of angle, force, and cut. In every game, too, your opponent's skill may change. In golf there is one thing to be done, and only one: to put a stationary ball into a stationary hole. And to do that one thing depends entirely upon yourself. Perhaps it is because you, and you alone, are to blame if you miss it, that you feel so keenly, so intensely, a fumbled stroke—another proof of the uniqueness of the game. To make a duck's egg at cricket is provoking enough. To lose one's queen at chess in depressing; though one always hopes to make up for it by phænomenal play with the rooks. To go into the net at tennis is disappointing, but the disappointment is apt to wear off with the rapidity of the set. To foozle at golf—how it *hurts!* I have seen my little caddie turn away, not in anger, nor in contempt, nor in reproach, but in pity. As to a multiplicity of foozles! pity the friends —and the foes—and the family—of that

To phoozle— how it worketh despite!

[104]

man who makes them, of all men most deject and wretched!

XXIV

How golf bewrays the character! You may know a man for years, yet discover new traits in him on the links. Characteristics long buried beneath convention are suddenly resuscitated; foibles sedulously suppressed spring into existence; hereditary instincts lying dormant reveal themselves. I was once for the first time made aware of the Hibernian origin of a partner by his antics over an astonishing put which won him the hole: for a moment of time his club might have been a shillelah, his feet moved to a jig. Golf brings out idiosyncrasies and peculiarities. Sometimes it brings out more than these! Hence, perhaps, the innumerability of the anecdotes anent the irrepressibility of profanity while

Golfe, it bewrayeth ye charactere;

And eftsones evoketh fearsome, yet withal scatheless, oathes,

playing the game—a game proverbially provocative of reprehensible expletives. My eyes were lately opened to this sinister peculiarity when playing with a man, the author of a ponderous work, noted for the precision, even for the purism, of his diction. Usually he spake as he wrote, and he wrote for gentlemen learned in the law. To my astonishment, one afternoon, far away in the windle straws on my right (we had diverged at the tee), proceeded from him the deepest and most earnest consignments to perdition of...whether it was himself, or his ball, or his iron, or the sum total of created things I did not distinctly understand. Not even had he a caddie in whose hearing to ejaculate. It was in the face of pure untainted Nature that he swore; and his deliberate damns sounded like bolts from the blue. Still, they comforted me. They proved to me, the duffer, that to take a foozle philosophically was not to be expected of mortal man. *And thus* Almost, I begin to think, a false stroke in *transcendeth* golf is more keenly felt than is a rejected *human* proposal. The girl may change her mind, *frailtie,* but a foozle is an irrevocable foozle, and a hole lost is lost forever. The inexorability of the game is appalling, and may well un-nerve the timorous player. Nothing in the rules of life and conduct is quite so rigid as are the conditions of this simple-seeming so-called "game." A hasty word may be re-called, a miscalculation corrected, a blun-der apologized for; but to no man is it given confidently to be able to say that he shall make up for a missed approach by a super-magnificent put. Master as a man is of his *And mocketh* muscles, on the links too often they seem *man his* the sport of chance. He may do his utmost; *foolysshe* exert himself to the sublimest limit of his *effortes;* ability; be cautious as a cat, alert as the lynx, and yet fail to place a simple round ball within three feet of a simple round hole, when only an easily computable number of paltry yards separate one from other. To no one is it given to say, "I shall play the next stroke well." That is curious. If one makes up one's mind to it, and is not thwarted, one can do most things well. How is it that the utmost deliberation, the extremest caution, the most scrupulous care, will often fail to put you where you would be? Almost it would seem that in golf is required that thing called amongst men "genius." One could no more undertake to produce a perfect put at every attempt than one could undertake to produce a perfect poem. Perhaps this is why the great masters of the art are held in such high esteem, an estimation never quite equalled by that accorded to their fellow-champions in, say, cricket or football. These are not, to my knowledge, asked by enterprising publishers to pose for their stance, or to supply photographs of their attitudes, or to give

And is in sooth unconquerable.

diagrammatic illustrations, drawn to scale, of their legs and arms. No; perhaps one of the profoundest secrets of the profound fascination exercised by golf lies in this, that, in spite of the fact that no one may thwart, oppose, or impede, there is no golfer living who could with surety assert that he will positively always do any particular hole in any particular number of strokes. Therein lies the irony of golf. The planets move in orbits exact as mathematics itself. The great balls of the universe are holed-out year by year with a precision which mocks our finest tools. Predict we can to the fraction of a second when Venus will approach the rim of the Sun, or Luna fall into the shadow of the Earth. But man, the master- *Analogues* mechanic of this terrestrial globe, versed in *astronomicall.* all the laws of parabola and ellipse, can no more govern the flight of his pigmy gutty than he can govern the flight of the summer swallow.

XXV

The ubiquitie
of golfe.

GOLF is unique, too, in that it can be played anywhere — on lone sea-shores or crowded heaths, over high-road and hedge, amid moss and weed, on the veldt, on the prairie, on the mead. (Obstacles are but "bunkers" to golf; the more the merrier. How encomiastic the St. Andrews golfer grows over his bunkers!) Certain links I know, far away on a western continent, a nine-hole course, miles from train or tram. Club-house there is none; you throw your covert coat and

Pourtraicture
of certaine
outlandisshe
lynkes.

your hat over a fence and — play. There are no greens, there are no flags: the player more familiar with the ground goes ahead and gives you the line. The teeing-grounds are marked by the spots where the soil has been scraped by the boot for the wherewithal for tees. Bunkers abound, and bad lies, in the form of hoof-marks and cart-ruts, do much more abound. Sheep and kine roam over them at will. For cooling drink after a heating round, you knock at a farm-house door for water. Yet to these links—and they are beautiful: high, hilly, green, a waving corn-field to your right, rolling pasture to your left, here and there a nodding coppice, and somnolent valleys variegating the scene—to these links daily gaily trudge ardent golfers, carrying clubs under a sub-arctic August sun—proof enough for me of the uniqueness of the game.

XXVI

AND yet it must be confessed that if this enthusiasm for the game were to be evoked in youths of sixteen or eighteen, and were strong enough to tempt them to forsake the crease or the goal for the links, not every one would applaud the lure. Not every one would be willing to see the youth of the

Howbeit, 'tis not a passtime for youthes.

United Kingdom of Great Britain and Ireland, or of the United States of America give up their national and traditional games. But there is no likelihood of such a catastrophe. For high spirits and supple joints golf is too sedate. Enthusiasts will play it world without end, as they have played it from time immemorial. And so, perhaps, will spirits that are losing the buoyancy and joints that are losing the suppleness of youth. But for the masses, golf to-day is a fashion, as much as was tennis a few years ago. To some this will be a hard saying, to others a consolatory one. The thought that his favourite links will some day be not so infested will perhaps give the confirmed and splenetic golfer heart of grace; the thought that his revered pass-time should be subject to fashion will wring from the confirmed and unsplenetic golfer hearty dissent. Yet that golf is a passing fashion I venture to assert. Cheap balls and iron clubs have put

Forsooth, golfe may prove a passant usage.

it within the reach of the many. And the
many, being usually a body of workers by
hand or brain, with only so much money,
time, and energy at their disposal, find in
this not-too-violent exercise a recreation
suited to their limitations. In golf, too, you
require only a single partner, not a team; a
match can be arranged by telephone in five
minutes, and can be finished between of-
fice-hours and dinner-time. But when the
links become a moving multitude resonant
with "'Fores!" when severe competition
raises record scores to a point which will kill
ambition in the novice and the amateur;
when 'Arry and 'Arriet take to afternoon
foursomes—as before long they will; why, *The vulgar*
then it is probable that the many who are *their golfe.*
not 'Arrys and 'Arriets will look about them
for less popular sports. All games, saving
only those national and traditional, have
their day; as witness: first, archery, then croquet, then tennis, and now golf. Within the

precincts of St. Andrews all this will be heresy. But St. Andrews will outlast fashion, as certainly it preceded fashion. Nor, I take it, would St. Andrews murmur if the popular fashion for golf did some day wane! How many balls already simultaneously encumber that classic ground? But all this very little concerns us here. Golf is in the very infancy of fashion, and will outlast many a generation yet.

Conjectures propounded concernynge fangles about to be.

What may take the place of golf when it ceases to be a fashion, it is hard to say. Archery, croquet, tennis, will never come in again. The bicycle is now an economic vehicle. Bowling-on-the-green is daily drawing devotees; but it cannot rival golf. Lacrosse is for the agile. Polo is expensive; so would be falconry. The dirigibility of the balloon is still a very long way off, in spite of MM. Maxim and Santos-Dumont; and at present not every one can afford to run the risk of being dumped five hundred miles from home. Aviation by æroplanes is for the few. Horse-racing and yachting are for kings or millionaires. Fencing is for the leisured and the cultured. Perhaps, when motor-cars come within measureable distance of possessivity, and roads are made, as Mr. H. G. Wells would have them, sensibly broad, we may see some startling sport. Speed is a tremendous intoxicant. When 'Arry can 'ire a heighty-'orsepower hauto, there will be fun — for 'Arry. — But were I to hazard a conjecture, I should be inclined to prophesy a wonderful future for rifle- *A prophecy* practice. The weapon is comparatively *hazarded.* cheap, so is the ammunition; Morris-tubes and sub-targets are easily erected, and ranges and butts ought to be as obtainable as links. Already rifle-clubs abound, and proficiency in musketry is yearly more highly esteemed — some twenty thousand people turned out to welcome home the King's Prizeman of 1904.

XXVII

Teachers of golfe do abound — as did Sophistes in times of eld.

BUT at the present moment golf is certainly as fashionable as unique, if we regard the mass of theoretical instruction proffered to the public, purporting to teach them how it should be played. Books, magazines, illustrations, photographs, diagrams, mathematical formulae, algebraic symbols, and rules without number, appear monthly. The swing, the stance, the address, the waggle — all are solemnly descanted upon. Why? Probably the true answer to this little question is as disingenuous as it will be disappointing. Cricket, football, tennis, racquets, and the rest, despite the adjectives "royal" and "ancient," are, to the masses, old; they were played by thousands long before the modern craze for scientific accuracy and analysis seized upon theoretic exponents of sport. Golf to the masses is comparatively new. Golf has been taken up by grey heads and stiff joints. And stiff joints and grey heads, unaccustomed to the swing proper to drivers and cleeks, require theoretic instruction. An eminent player and elucidator of the game, expatiating on the multiplicity of the coexisting styles of play, looks forward to the time when some more rigid and scientific analysis of stroke shall be possible, and when some fixed and ideal form shall be evolved. Personally, I look forward to the *Ye efficacie* time when all these elaborate directions as *of such* to the precise manner in which some *teachynge* twenty-seven and a half drachms avoirdu- *questioned.* pois of gutta-percha shall be propelled some two hundred yards shall be regarded as a curious characteristic of a bygone age. Some two thousand years ago Aristotle had the temerity to affirm that the lyre was learned by playing the lyre. Some two thousand years hence some golfer may have the temerity to affirm that golf is learned by playing golf. In proof of which rash assertion I here adduce an illustration as simple and as disappointing as, I feel, is my predic-tion. There is at my club a little caddie, by name Willie Dobson (note the name, I pray you; it may some day be inscribed on as many clubs as is now the name of Willie Dunn). Willie Dobson just now weighs be-tween five and six stone, measures about four foot two, and is aged *circiter* thirteen years. He has not read Mr. Horace Hutch-inson or William Parkes, junior, or Herd, or Mr. Low, or Mr. Beldam; he knows not the Badminton Series; he is all unaware that Vardon and Braid have become scribes as

A wondrous caddie.

well as champions of the game; he has not heard of "advanced golf"; he has not stud-ied instantaneous photographs of distin-guished drivers, approachers, and putters; and I seriously doubt whether he has prac-ticed before a mirror. The Bogey for my links, as computed by a careful committee for grown-up men, is eighty-one. Well,

The Abundance of Instruction

Willie has done them in eighty-five, and can do them again. Half a century hence he will be asked to write a book on golf. Would I could read it!—To conclude. Did we all commence golf as Willie Dobson has commenced it, there would be little need of rule or rote. Willie Dobson learned golf by caddying for a St. Andrews golfer.

Not but that, I am fully prepared to admit, there is absolute necessity for commencing the game properly. Perhaps another feature in the uniqueness of golf is that, in it, style counts for so much, so very much. So long as you play with a straight bat you may run up a score at cricket with a poor style; but already in golf I have met men who, by some unaccountable trick of style, had so far got out of the particular knack of the drive, that they had perforce to tee off with a cleek. How many beginners, too, are "off" their irons to-day and "off" their wooden clubs to-morrow! However, I

Of style: that is of forme or manere.

take it these mishaps occur rather to the grey-headed and stiff-jointed beginners than to Willie Dobsons or Willie Dunns; although W. Fernie's lamentable performance at Prestwich, in 1887, is a warning even to the expert. Up almost to the days of the championship match, we are told, he was playing in perfect form; during the contest he heeled ball after ball.

XXVIII

In golfe, 'tis the minde that excelleth.

FEW things shew so clearly the influence of the mind upon the body as the game of golf. The links, I have sometimes thought, might not seldom with advantage be exchanged for the laboratory by both professors and students of experimental psychology. For example, I have it on very direct evidence, namely, from one of the contestants himself, that one of the greatest matches in the history of golf was in

all probability decided on psychological
grounds alone. Between the opponents
there was little, if any, disparity of skill; but
one had the advantage of strength and experience. By means of the first qualification
he again and again outdrove his antagonist;
by means of the second he retained un-
shaken, throughout the five days' arduous
struggle, his judgment and his nerve. The *A proofe*
consequence was, so more than one specta- *thereof.*
tor averred, that the younger adversary was
tempted to "press"; and the inevitable and
fatal consequence of pressing was loss of
accuracy and ultimate defeat. How many
golfers, too, either resent or welcome the
existence of a "gallery." If there is nothing *Of*
in golf but a test of strength and skill, what *"galleries"*
should matter the presence or the absence *—so ynamed.*
of some few score on-looking human folk?
What cricketer at Lord's or the Oval gives a
thought to the Pavilion? Yet some men a
gallery disconcerts, others it stimulates. As-

suredly this influence is psychic. The fact is that the judgment and the delicacy requisite in golf are so extreme, so fine, that the minutest perturbation of the mind, and therefore of the brain, and therefore of the whole nervous system by which the action of the muscles is controlled, affects the accuracy of the stroke. It would be interesting to attach sphygmographs to various golfers, both phlegmatic and mercurial, and to compare the tracings under the varying conditions of the game, — though probably even the pulse-beats are a less delicate criterion of mental equanimity or perturbation than are the drive, the approach, and the put. A famous Italian experimental psychologist, by name Angelo Mosso, has recently proved, by means of a nicely balanced instrument, that each and every varying condition of the mind produces a corresponding variation in the circulation of the blood. Just such another nicely balanced instru-

Suggestiouns chirurgique.

Signor Mosso, his device.

ment is golf. (Was it not a famous — or an infamous — golfer who was once upset by the singing of a da...of a dastardly lark?) The merest tyro soon discovers something of this. Perhaps this is why the tyro is so particular to enquire as to what he should eat and what he should drink and how-withal he should be clothed. —

To the on-looker these minutiæ are, of course, highly amusing. But the amused on-looker little knows on what minute things great golfing matters sometimes turn. There is a fatefulness about golf that is ter-rorizing. Momentous events often enough hang upon the minutest causes. But nothing even in the realm of the physical sciences is more inexorable or rigid than golf. The centre of gravity of the solid earth, so they tell us, is altered by a footstep. That is con-ceivable, though it is not perceptible. Yet with my own eyes have I seen a great match between two rival clubs, with twenty players

Of smallen thynges, how that they doe count for moche.

*How litling
a thynnge
will worke
huge mischefe*

a side, determined by a two-foot put missed at the eighteenth hole. And did not Alexander Herd, in that extraordinary tournament of the Professional Golfers' Association on the Mid-Surrey links, at Richmond Old Deer-Park, in 1904, just fail of actually defeating Braid, Vardon, and Taylor in succession, by a less than two-foot put missed at the seventeenth hole? I have known a club championship to depend upon a stymie at the nineteenth hole. "What will you give us?" said once one pair in a foursome to the other. "O, a stroke on the nineteenth hole," was the jocular reply. By that stroke, by the grimness of fate, that match was decided. — The veteran golfer thinks on these things and ponders them in his heart; and little he recks of the amusement or the derision of the on-looker. *Mathematica mathematicis scribuntur.*

*Golfe — 'tis
an esoterique
sporte.*

It may be that the recital of such mistakes as these, made by eminent golfers, is, on the whole, somewhat of a consolation to the *Historicall* duffer, to him to whom, for the time being, *mis-haps,* golf seems little more than a series of mis- *how solacing* takes. And so it may be. And the recital *they ben.* might be abundantly amplified. The champion of a hemisphere once missed the winning of a pewter by taking eleven for a hundred-and-seventy-five-yard hole in which no bunker intervened between teeing ground and putting green; a hole which he usually accomplished in three, sometimes in two.* And I once saw one of the most expert of lady golfers, when playing against the lady champion of a great colony, land twice in succession in a water-jump in making a thirty-yard approach, when the lie was perfect, she was three feet from the stream,

*It should be told, however, that the course was extremely narrow, and that a horrible ravine skirted the green. The player in question drove out of bounds twice, and then into the horrible ravine.

An incident most calamitous.

and the ground was flat!—Yes, such things are consoling to us all. To err is human, even on the links.

I have sometimes thought, too, that I could detect a curious psychic contagion on the links. It is within every golfer's experi-

Diversitie of players.

ence that he finds he plays well against certain opponents and badly against others; and this, not so much on account of the quality of his opponent's game as on account of his temperament or character. You are steadied by one man, you are upset by another; this opponent hurries you and harries you, the other unwittingly calls out your better self. This is highly curious—and highly significant, being indeed one more proof of the fact that in this game, which outwardly and to the inexperienced seems merely a test of skill and strength, there is in reality some unimaginable and unsearchable contest between some inner and innominable centres in the combatants. For it

[126]

is not his mere trick of manner that makes one man antipathetic to another on the links; it is something far more deep-seated than this: it is something inherent in the innermost recesses of his nature, something intangible, invisible, arcanal. Is there some inscrutable medium between soul and soul, the existence of which only golf reveals? I recommend the links as a fruitful field for the experiments of the thought-reader, or the investigations of the Society for Psychical Research.

Phantasticall antipathies.

XXIX

GOLF, indeed, is a fruitful field of psychological phænomena. For example, hypnotists of the most modern school aver, I believe, that there exist somewhere in the brain or mind of man five distinct layers of consciousness. For proofs of multiple consciousness the hypnotist should frequent the

Of "hypnotisme"— so-ycleped.

links. He will there often find one layer of consciousness roundly upbraiding another, sometimes in the most violent language of abuse, for a foozled stroke; and so earnest sometimes is the vituperation poured by the unmerciful abuser upon the unfortunate foozler, that truly one is apt sometimes sincerely to commiserate the former, and to regard him as the victim of a multiple personality, and not at all blameable for his own poor play. Golfers, too, have I known who imagine themselves constantly accompanied by a sort of Socratic *daimon* prompting them to this, that, or the other method of manipulating the club—without doubt a mystic manner of looking upon one's *alter ego*. It would be interesting to "suggest" to a duffer, while in the cataleptic trance, to keep his eye on the ball, and to follow through, and then to watch the result. If these fundamental rules (so easy to preach, so difficult to practice) could be relegated to some au-

Selfe-accusatioun—how droll withal it be.

tomatic sub-stratum of consciousness, leaving the higher centres free to judge of distance and direction (for it is thus, probably, that the man who has golfed from childhood plays), the task of many a professional might be simplified. All of which goes to show that, in the game of golf, the mind plays a larger part than, in many quarters, is apt to be imagined.

The physiological explanation of the preponding influence of mind over body in golf is this: Precise coördination of hand and eye is necessary; this coördination is directed by nerve currents (cerebral and cerebro-spinal) conveyed to the muscles; which nerve-currents depend for their regularity upon the mind. Unless the supreme and regulating centres of intelligence, wherein lie imbedded the cells from which orders for muscular movement derive, are, first, in thorough working order, and, second, intent upon the business in hand, the or-

Proofe of ye potencie of minde.

ders conveyed through the delicate efferent nerve-fibres governing the equally delicate muscular fibres of the fingers, hands, wrists, legs, and arms, will be ineffectual, and the resulting stroke inaccurate. In short it would seem that a man, to play golf well, must play like a machine; but like a machine in which the mental motor must be as perfect as the muscular mechanism.

XXX

"Kinæsthe-sis," what a queynte thynge it be:

PERHAPS the sense most prominently brought into play in golf is that to which I have already referred and which is known to physiologists as kinæsthesis or the "muscular sense"—the sixth sense, as it is sometimes called. By the muscular sense it is that we calculate the exact amount of force required for a particular posture or movement. It is by this sense that we wield so deftly the knife and fork, the spoon, and the pen. To keep a bouncing ball bouncing just *Expositioun* so high, requires just such a tap and no *thereof.* more. That tap is regulated by the muscular sense. To poise an ounce weight on the tips of the fingers requires just such relative rigidity of the phalangeal flexors and extensors. Double the resilience of the bouncing-ball, or poise two ounces instead of one, and the taps or the muscular rigidity must immediately be changed, the amount of change being regulated by the muscular sense. Now, in ordinary life this sense is exercised only within very narrow limits, and is rarely, if ever, called upon to judge of great distances. It carries food to the mouth; it raises a hat; it is skilled in

"The nice conduct of a clouded cane";

it may occasionally throw a stone at a dog or a boot-jack at a cat; but it does little more. Some games exercise it more than others. In cricket it is highly valuable; in

[131]

tennis and racquets even more so. Rowing utilizes it but little. In baseball you hit, and in football you kick, as hard as you can. In croquet it is important. But in croquet all

Variablenesse of its duetees. the strokes are the same. But in golf! In golf, within the space of ten minutes, it is called upon to drive two hundred yards; loft another hundred; and put five inches. In golf you have strokes that require the strength of a slog in cricket, combined with the delicacy of cup-and-ball. In golf you get the whole gamut of the muscular sense, from the gigantic swipe at the tee to the gentle tap on the green. It is called into play at every stroke, and it differs with every difference of club — its weight, its length of shaft, the angle which its face subtends to the horizon, its rigidity or flexibility, the construction and material of its head. — Golf, in short, is a sort of Gargantuan jugglery, a prodigious prestidigitation, a Titanic thimble-rigging, a mighty legerdemain.

XXXI

AMONG the psychological aspects of golf is its effect upon the character; and this is neither small nor unimportant. There is no more inexorable an opponent than your links. Implacable as fate, they exact to the uttermost farthing for the minutest divergence from the narrow path. Atropos will sooner be turned aside than they. Your mortal foe may relent, may show mercy; in golf, between first tee and home hole look thou not for changeableness nor shadow of turning. And for peccant man this is good. It is disciplinary. Whom golf loveth it chasteneth; and few men but come off the course, be it on the first round or the five-hundredth, chastened, and by consequence strengthened. Even victory fails to puff up, for victory always is hardly won, and always it is not your natural, but your human, foe that is defeated. Your natural foe, with his

Golfe, a medicament for ye caractere.

[133]

hazards and his bunkers still unharmed and threatening, still grimly smiles, still challenges you to completer conquest. For, in short, your links are invincible. Could you hole out in one on every drive the holes would be only halved, and you and they would come out but even all. For *space* is the one eternal and immutable enemy of man. It is to conquer space that we resort to steam and electricity, the penny-post and the tram-car, the motor and the bicycle, the brassey, the cleek. So that, even if you brought every hole within holing distance of every drive, the necessity of that drive would prove the necessity of that effort to overcome space. It would be an attractive, but perhaps a too transcendental, thought to imagine that in some future, supralunary, n-dimensional world, this infinite enemy, space, will at last be worsted. There the tee-ing-ground will be identical with the putting-green, the drive one with the put, the

A briefe ex-cursus as to Space:

Man, his supernall enemie.

[134]

hole coincident with the tee. There achievement will be accomplished without effort, attainment will be identical with endeavour, the ideal will be the real. That will be on beatific links indeed, where room for bunkers will be none.

XXXII

FOR not even against Bogey is it that even on this spatial and temporal world you pit your strength. Bogey is but a human compromise between erring man and unerring Nature; an ideal player, an apotheosized golfer, and anthropomorphic deity of the links. Bogey is that great exemplar whom, despairing of overcoming great Nature herself, we each strive to imitate, even to excel. He is the player who is never off his game; is always in training; never makes a mistake; never loses his temper or his head; whom no defeat dejects and no victory elates; who is imperturbable, persistent, placid. In golf,

How that Bogey (so it be callen) is not the trewe combatant against whom ye golfer warreth.

as in life, frail and mortal man is brought into conflict with sempiternal Nature. His pigmy strength, his uncertain skill, are arrayed against the immutable, the inexpugnable. And as we may say that all evolution, all progress, all development have come about solely because of unceasing combat with unyielding Nature; that man is *How serious* not now an ape, and the ape is not now a *a thynge,* mollusc, because of that fight with cosmic *golfe it be!* force; so we may see in golf something of the same struggle, with its fortifying influences on character. And golf is good for the character in many ways. It is serious as life. It admits no peccadillos; it permits no compromises; it recognizes no venial sins. A false step, a scarce perceptible slip, — and you are lost. There is nothing to complain of in the conditions. The laws of the game are simple as the decalogue. Abstract and absolute justice is meted out to you. If you fail, it is you who are culpable and none other. But it is in this very simplicity and rigidity of law that there lies concealed, for aspiring and progressive man, the subtlest lure.

XXXIII

AFTER all, what leads you on in golf is this. You think a perfect pitch of excellence can be attained. But that pitch of excellence continually recedes the nearer you approach it. Intellectual apprehension outruns physical achievement. Accordingly, the allurement is unceasing, and the fascination endless. Always you can imagine a longer drive, a more accurate approach, a more certain put; never, or rarely ever, do you effect all three at every hole in the course. But all men—who are golfers—always live in hopes of accomplishing them. The conditions never vary; the obstacles remain always the same; the thing to be done to-day is precisely that which was to be done yes-

The verie lure of golfe.

terday, last year; and as man never is, but always to be, blessed, as hope springs eternal in the human breast, as progress, as development, is the one incontestable instinct implanted in all things living, the cosmic principle, the law of heaven and earth, the motive of all effort, the germ of all action —the phantom of perfect success flits ever before the ardent golfer. And what golfer ever was there who was not ardent?

XXXIV

To excell is hard to come atte.

How comes it about, then, that, if the conditions are so simple, success is so difficult? The fact is, there is enormous *chance* in golf. There must be, when you propel a cubic inch of gutta-percha over acres of soil. Were the links a gigantic billiard-table, chance might to a certain extent be eliminated, as no doubt in billiards it actually is. But the links being what they are, namely, some two or three square miles of open country, variegated in its every square inch, in any one square inch of which you may lie, and each square inch of which may affect differently the character of your stroke or the roll of your ball, chance, to the beginner in golf, we may safely compute as infinite. But, as one improves, the conditions being fixed and determined, skill directly eliminates chance. In no other game is the equipoise between chance and skill so exact, since in all other games a third and variable factor enters into the problem, the skill, namely, of your opponent. In nothing, perhaps, is the perennial fascination of golf so plainly to be found as in this direct ratio between the increment of skill and the corresponding decrement of chance. We may put it thus: —

> Let a = skill, and
> Let x = chance; then
> x varies from ∞ to 0 as
> a varies from 0 to ∞.

Of chaunce.

That is, when the skill is zero, chance is infinite; when (if ever) skill is infinite, chance will be zero. There is no likelihood of any links losing their charm through the entire elimination of chance by reason of superlative skill. Golf will never become a hazardous, outdoor billiards. It will take a million years to develope the muscular sense to such a pitch as that it will land the ball, after a hundred yards' flight, plumb on a given point, free from all cups, on a perfect lie — though, from the annually improving records for several links, the muscular sense is evidently tending that way.

XXXV

AND now, wherein lies the supreme mystery of this so-called "game"? In this surely, that whereas the thing to be done seems most easy of accomplishment, it is as a matter of physical and metaphysical fact a feat requiring the deftest use of the most delicate mechanism. Mind (or matter, which you will) in the long course of its evolution from amœba to man, has as yet, so far as we know, here upon this planet produced nothing more complex in structure than the human neural apparatus; and it is this apparatus, in its most secret recesses, that is called into requisition by every player at every stroke. And whereas the thing to be done is rigidly fixed, but the anatomical machinery by which it is to be done is capable, humanly speaking, of infinite improvement, the pitch of excellence at which we aim continually recedes the farther we advance, and we are lured on, and lured on... to the delight of professionals and caddies, to the pecuniary profit of club stewards and manufacturers of expensive balls, but to the sorrow of waiting wives and to the scorn of maledictory onlookers.

The writer returneth to his theme, & essayeth to determine wherein lieth trewely the mysterie of golfe.

We can put no limit, humanly speaking, to the possibilities of the neural system.

Anatomicall problemes.

What the brain, the spinal cord, the nerves, and the muscles may not some day be capable of achieving, we cannot say; and to what pitch of perfection the associative memory may be trained it is equally impossible to determine. And every golfer feels in himself these possibilities of improvement. Intellectual apprehension, I have said, outruns physical achievement. Every golfer, that is, knows precisely and definitely what it is he is called upon to do; but he feels that the machinery by which it is to be done may be indefinitely improved—if only he can discover how to improve it. Accordingly every golfer strenuously endeavours to improve it. "It can be done; I can do it"; so every golfer says to himself—he *will* do it, by the Styx he declares he will.—The professional of my links once went round in the magnificent score of sixty-six. Upon my congratulating him, what was his reply? "Well, sir, I missed three putts. I can do it in sixty-three."

The minde, it transcendeth the bodie.

The Socratique theorie of σοφία *versus Aristotle his theorie of* ἕξις.

The Supreme Mystery

Some day he will,* and then no doubt he will say, "Well, sir, I missed so-and-so. I can do it in sixty-one." — Will he rest content then? Of course not. And the same spirit urges on the veriest duffer. *Ane other tale.*

The curious thing is that this extraordinary ambition seems to appertain solely to golf. On every round every golfer strains every nerve to break his own record. Nor is there any other game in which defeat is so poignantly felt. Why? We must fall back on the theory that it is because the thing to be done seems so simple, so patently, so palpably simple, that everybody thinks he ought to be able to do it, and *therefore* defeat rankles — rankles. Were it hugely difficult; did it require the superlative development of this, that, or the other intellectual or physical faculty, we should succumb with a good grace — as we do when we play with an ac- *The golfer his unweting ambitioun.*

---

*I believe he has since done it in sixty-three.

Defeat att golfe—how pitifulle it be!

knowledged expert, say, of chess, or billiards, or whist, or whatnot. But in golf to succumb with a good grace is to acknowledge that in the very fibre and essence of the man who beats us there is something to which we cannot attain.—Which seems one more proof of the fact that in golf it is the very fibre and essence of a man that count; not mere power, or knack, or agility. And no doubt this is true. How many games have been won by indomitableness of spirit alone; how many by a quiet self-confidence; how many by a reserve and a restraint that can watch with perfect equanimity hole after hole won by unwonted brilliancy, and yet win by dogged and determined adhesion to steady play?

XXXVI

FROM all this is there anything practical to be learned? I am afraid not. If you have golfed from childhood, you will laugh at it;

if you have taken up golf at forty, it will not be of much use to you. The youthful caddie, whose cortical centres are in a docile stage and who accordingly picks up the game by sheer imitation, and the elderly professional, who has done nothing but make clubs and swing them all his life, probably play almost automatically — as you or I wield a knife and fork, a spoon, or a pen. To the one, golf is what gambols are to the kitten; to the other, what mousing is to the cat. Not theirs to analyse the method of their play. I know a professional who says that in reality there is only one stroke in the game in which he has to keep in mind one little rule, namely, to play off the right foot in a hanging lie. How different from the amateur novice! I was playing the other day with a University professor, a charming man and an erudite. He happened to be off his drive, and at the fifteenth tee (a sequestered spot), with a sort of despairing

And yet, alack! in all this pother ther be little of profitte.

cry to heaven, he muttered as he took his stance, "Now, I wonder whether I *can* for once keep my eye on the ball and follow through?" He did not even attempt to burthen his University brain with more than two, and these elementary, injunctions.

The veritable *probleme.*

"But can you not tell us," I can readily understand the reader—by this time no doubt (and quite legitimately) impatient— saying, "can you not tell us what it really is at bottom that wins in golf? What is the one thing needful? What is the pearl of great price? What is the great and important factor of success?"—My dear sir, would to heaven that I could! If I could tell myself, most gladly would I tell you.—However, upon one thing I presume all golfers will be agreed, upon this, namely: that, *all other things being equal* (but they never are), what wins is *dexterity.* Given two golfers absolutely evenly matched in character, temperament, and strength; both equally self-confident,

collected, and careful; and victory will fall
to the more dexterous. Other things being
equal, if you can drive and approach and *Golfe and*
put as easily and effortlessly as a facile *writynge—*
writer dots his *i*'s and crosses his *t*'s, you *and musick.*
will win. There is no doubt about that. Golf
is like writing with a crowbar. If Monsieur
Paderewski could play golf as he plays
Liszt's Sixth Rhapsodie Hongroise, nobody
could beat him; for in those rapid semi-
demi-semiquaver staccato octaves Paderewski combines a strength with a dexterity marvellous to witness. But, curiously
enough, in golf dexterity seems to count
even more than strength. I have seen a su- *Of dexteritie,*
perb little lady golfer, who assuredly could *its potencie.*
not have had more than nineteen birthdays,
and who I am quite sure tipped the scales
well under nine stone, drive ball after ball
clean and straight, some just under, some
over, two-hundred yards—to the delight
and the admiration and the adoration of

great male golfers in the gallery. That was due surely to the dexterity with which she made use of all the strength she possessed.

Ane other fayre one: how laudable she ben;

At the moment when her club met her ball, every ounce of weight and every foot-pound of energy she could command were communicated to the ball, without altering by a hair's breadth the even rhythm of her swing or the faultless precision of her stance —nay, more, she put her whole heart and soul into the stroke as well; and these counted for much, very much. (If you wish to know for how much, I will tell you: at the eighth green I saw her pick up her oppo-

And eke how loveable.

nent's ball, take a big piece of mud off it, and smilingly replace it. That showed the sportsman's heart and soul!) All I can say is, Go thou and do likewise. Ah! many were the grown men and women in that gallery who wished that they could!

Yes; I take it it is the consummate combination of strength and dexterity that—the

[148]

psychological factors being eliminated—ultimately win. You may have the strength of
an ox; but unless you have also the agility of
a cat it will avail you little. Unless you can
drive straight and judge distance to a nicety,
mere length is nought. Yet on the other
hand, unless you can cover a great deal of
ground on your long game, even extreme
accuracy on your short game is heavily
handicapped. But the real and most effective combination is that of immense power
with extreme delicacy. Therein lies the mystery of golf, so far as the mere bodily frame
is concerned. It consists just in this, that you
can wield a driver weighing a pound just as
easily and as surely as you can a penholder
weighing a drachm; that you can use your
strongest muscles—almost every muscle in
your body at once—at their extremest limit
as easily and surely as you sign your name.
—I am cock-sure my Pro can approach a
hole better than he can sign his name. But,

*Ye consum-
mation: it
consisteth in
strength &
skille.*

[149]

as we have seen, this effective combination of strength and skill is itself the result of some mysterious and inner psychic centres forever inscrutable to man.

XXXVII

One Messer
Mill cited.

JOHN STUART MILL once anxiously debated whether there would not come a time when all the tunes possible with the five tones and two semi-tones of the octave would be exhausted. So, many a non-golfing wife and unsympathising onlooker thinks there surely must come a time when the erring husband and friend will tire of trudging over the country trying to put half-crown balls into four-and-a-half-inch holes.

But to little
purport.

The outsider does not know that at every hole is enacted every time a small but intensely interesting three-act drama.* There

---

*I gratefully acknowledge my indebtedness for the germ of this idea to a capital article by "T.P." in *M.A.P.*

is Act I, the Drive, with its appropriate mise-en-scène: the gallery, the attendant caddies, the toss for the honour. At long holes it is a long act if we include the brassey shots. There is Act II, the Approach. This is what the French call the *nœud* of the plot: much depends on the Approach. And the mise-en-scène is correspondingly enhanced in interest: the lie, the hazard, the wind, the character of the ground—all become of increasing importance. There is Act III, the Put. It also has its back-ground, its "business," and its "properties": the caddie at the flag, the irregularities of the green, the peculiarities of the turf, the possibilities of a stymie.— Eighteen dramas, some tragical, some farcical, in every round; and in every round protagonist and deuteragonist constantly interchanging parts. No wonder the ardent golfer does not tire of his links, any more than the ardent musician tires of his notes.

Dramaticall analogues.

What theatre-goer enjoys such plays? And
what staged plays have such a human interest in them? And, best of all, they are acted
in the open air, amid delightful scenery, with
the assurance of healthy exercise and pleas-
ant companionship. What theatre-goer enjoys such plays?—And when the curtain
is rung down and the eighteenth flag re-
placed, instead of a cigar in a hansom, or
a whisky-and-soda at a crowded bar, or a
snack at a noisy grill-room, there is the amicable persiflage in the dressing-room or the
long quiet talk on the veranda.

*The writer
discourseth
of his lynkes,
their beau-
semblance.*

Nor does the golfer ever tire of the stage
upon which these his out-door dramas are
played.—I have been promising myself
time and again to go round some day, un-
armed with clubs and carrying no balls, for
the express purpose of seeing and enjoying
in detail the beauties of my links. There are
some woods fringing portions of the course
most tempting to explore, woods in which I

get glimpses of lovable things, and a wealth of colour which for its very loveliness I forgive for hiding my sliced ball. There are deep ravines—alack! I know them well—where, between lush grass edges trickles a tiny rill, by the quiet banks of which, but for the time-limit, I should loiter long. There is a great breezy hill, bespattered with humble plants, to traverse the broad back of which almost tempts to slice and to pull. A thick boscage, too, whereon the four seasons play a quartet on the theme of green, and every sun-lit day composes a symphony beautiful to behold. And there are nooks, and corners, and knolls, and sloping lawns on which the elfish shadows dance. Smells too, curious smells, from noonday pines, and evening mists, from turf, and fallen leaves. ... What is it these things *say?* Whither do they beckon? What do they reveal? I seem to be listening to some cosmic obligato the while I play; a great and unheard melody

swelling from the great heart of Nature. —
Every golfer knows something of this. But,
as Herodotus says, these be holy things
whereof I speak not. *Favete linguis.*

XXXVIII

The joye of combatte.

Lastly, let us not omit to include amongst
the elements of the fascination which golf
wields over its votaries that *gaudium certaminis,** that joy of contest, which always the
game evokes. It is one of the chief ingredients of the game, and it is evoked and re-
evoked at every point of the game, from the
initial drive to the ultimate put. It is an ingredient of every manly sport is this "warrior's stern joy," but in golf it is paramount
and overt. Every stroke arouses it, for the
exact value of every stroke is patent to both
player and opponent. Few other games keep

*Thank you, W.H.B., for this hint.

the inborn masculine delight in sheer struggle at so high a pitch. No wonder the stakes in golf are merely nominal; no wonder that often there are no stakes at all; the keenness of the rivalry is stimulus enough. — And this, surely, is one of the chief beauties of the game. It will never be spoiled by the intrusion of professionalism; at least it will never be played by highly-paid professionals for the delectation of a howling and betting mob; nor, thank heavens, will rooters ever sit on fences and screech at its results. At present it is uncontaminated by either "bookies" or "bleachers"; nay, it has not yet reached that stage in its history when it asks for gate-money.

XXXIX

BUT the ultimate analysis of the mystery of golf is hopeless — as hopeless as the ultimate analysis of that of metaphysics or of *The writer admitteth his nescience.*

that of the feminine heart. Fortunately the hopelessness as little troubles the golfer as it does the philosopher or the lover. The *summum bonum* of the philosopher, I suppose, is to evolve a nice little system of metaphysics of his own. The *summum bonum* of the lover is of course to get him a nice little feminine heart of his own. Well, the *summum bonum* of the golfer is to have a nice little private links of his own (and, now-a-days, perhaps, a private manufactory of rubber-cored balls into the bargain), and to be able to go round his private links daily, accompanied by a professional and a caddie. — It would be an interesting experiment to add to these a psychologist, a leech, a chirurgeon, a psychiater, an apothecary, and a parson.

Recommendaciouns.

XL

To sum up, then, in what does the secret of golf lie? Not in one thing; but in many. And

in many so mysteriously conjoined, so in-
comprehensibly interwoven, as to baffle
analysis. The mind plays as large a part as
the muscles; and perhaps the moral nature
as large a part as the mind—though this
would carry us into regions deeper even
than these depths of psychology. Suffice it
to say that all golfers know that golf must be
played seriously, earnestly; as seriously, as
earnestly, as life.

Conclusion—
inne whilke,
par fay, no
thingen ben
concluded.

XLI

BUT may not also the simple delights of the
game and its surroundings, with their effect
upon the mind and the emotions, be in-
cluded under the allurements and the mystery of golf? My knowledge of links up to
the present is limited, but on mine there are
delights which, to me a duffer, are like Pis-
gah sights: hills, valleys, trees, a gleaming
lake in the distance, a grand and beloved

Golfe, the
lowlie delites
thereof.

piece of bunting lending gorgeous colour to the scene; a hospitable club-house with spacious verandas and arm-chairs; shower-baths; tea and toast; whisky and soda; genial companionship; and the ever-delectable

Of diverse delectable thynnges; and

pipe. Has anyone yet sung these delights of the game? the comradeship in sport, the friendliness, the community of sentiment, the frankness of speech, the good-will, the "generosity in trifles"? Or of the links themselves? the great breeze that greets you on the hill, the whiffs of air — pungent, penetrating — that come through green things growing, the hot smell of pines at noon, the wet smell of fallen leaves in autumn, the damp and heavy air of the valleys at eve, the lungs full of oxygen, the sense of freedom on a great expanse, the exhilaration,

Of beautie.

the vastness, the buoyancy, the exaltation? ... And how beautiful the vacated links at dawn, when the dew gleams untrodden beneath the pendant flags and the long shadows lie quiet on the green; when no caddie intrudes upon the still and silent lawns, and you stroll from hole to hole and drink in the beauties of a land to which you know you will be all too blind when the sun mounts high and you toss for the honour!

AFTERWORD

by John Updike

HE TEXT you have just pe-
rused is that of the first edition
of *The Mystery of Golf,* pub-
lished in 1908 in a limited edition of only four hundred and forty copies.
The book's unexpected success prompted
the publication two years later of a second,
enthusiastically expanded edition, to which
Arnold Haultain added a hundred addi-
tional pages of text, thickening the already
rich texture of the prose with yet more
quaint learning and fancy writing, with
more foreign phrases, leisurely ruminations,
metaphysical and physiological lore, and
references to such worthies as Saint Paul,
Tennyson, and Yrjö Hirn. Houghton Miff-

lin has wisely decided to republish the earlier, shorter text, in which Haultain's few basic points are already more than sufficiently elaborated in the half-facetious, generously allusive style of turn-of-the-century essayistic writing.

We have here material for a solid short article finespun into a charming little book. Its core, however, is pure gold; with an analytical ardor that, as he says, only a tyro of mature years could have mustered (for the young beginner would not be so analytical, and the seasoned player not quite so ardent), Haultain goes to the heart of golf's peculiar lovability and enduring fascination. His shrewdest point comes early, in section V, and bears repeating:

> ... there is no other game in which these three fundamental factors—the physiological, the psychological, and the social or moral—are so extraordinarily [the

second edition substitutes the more telling adverb "intimately"] combined or so constantly called into play. . . . In no other game that I know of is, first, the whole anatomical frame brought into such strenuous yet delicate action at every stroke; or, second, does the mind play so important a part in governing the actions of the muscles; or, third, do the character and temperament of your opponent so powerfully affect you as they do in golf. To play well, these three factors in the game must be most accurately adjusted, and their accurate adjustment is as difficult as it is fascinating.

In no other sport, that is, does the player so continuously and closely have to perform as his own coach. "Every stroke," Haultain tells us, "must be played by the mind— gravely, quietly, deliberately." In no other sport are mental effort and concentration so immediately reflected in the mirror of physical action and its result. The tennis player crouched on the back line, the baseball pitcher on the mound certainly exhort themselves and inwardly rehearse some technical points; but they can also depend to a large degree upon natural ability and instilled reflex. Golf, it seems, must be learned afresh each time we tee off, and if on the one hand it humbles us with a sudden collapse of some aspect of play we thought had been mastered, it on the other always holds out, perhaps even more to the inept than to the expert, the hope of dramatic improvement. Haultain lucidly extols the fluid, multiform, neo-Platonic complexity of golf as a mental and — though his recurring emphasis on moral fibre as well as mental focus will strike us as old-fashioned — spiritual experience.

Those who can, do; and those who cannot, theorize. Out of his presumed embarrassments in practice Haultain developed a profound grasp of golf's lovely tensions. The chronic debate over whether the stroke is a swing or a hit is resolved in this sentence, worthy of memorization: "It is in fact a subtile combination of a swing and a hit; the 'hit' portion being deftly incorporated into the 'swing' portion just as the head of the club reaches the ball, yet without disturbing the regular rhythm of the motion." He troubles to express, too, the elegant paradox of the starkly simple objective toward which golf's many tools and advisements and wayward incidents all tend: "to knock a ball into a hole—that seems the acme of ease." The late nineteenth century's Darwinian obsessions sharpened Haultain's awareness of the elemental combat beneath golf's genteel formalities—combat in which the human opponent is only the secondary enemy, the primary foe being "great Nature herself" in the guise of the course. He is an eloquent poet of the golf course, and his concluding paragraph is rapturous:

> But may not also the simple delights of the game and its surroundings, with their effect upon the mind and the emotions, be included under the allurements and the mystery of golf? My knowledge of links up to the present is limited, but on mine there are delights which, to me a duffer, are like Pisgah sights: hills, valleys, trees, a gleaming lake in the distance . . . the great breeze that greets you on the hill, the whiffs of air—pungent, penetrating—that come through green things growing, the hot smell of pines at noon, the wet smell of fallen leaves in autumn, the damp and heavy air of the valleys at eve, the lungs full of oxygen, the sense of freedom on a great expanse, the exhilaration, the vastness, the buoyancy, the exaltation . . . And how beautiful the vacated links at dawn, when the

dew gleams untrodden beneath the pendant flags and the long shadows lie quiet on the green; when no caddie intrudes upon the still and silent lawns, and you stroll from hole to hole and drink in the beauties of a land to which you know you will be all too blind when the sun mounts high and you toss for the honour!

Haultain has proven not quite correct in his prophecy that golf "will never be spoiled by professionalism; at least it will never be played by highly-paid professionals for the delectation of a howling and betting mob." The mobs do not (unless the Ryder Cup is at stake) howl, but they sigh and cheer, and tournament courses have added bleachers, and gate-money is part of the deal. His sense of golf as an exhilarating combat with an untamable Nature might be dulled, I fear, by a look at today's new courses, with their watered and weed-

less fairways, flowerbed-lined tees, and em-
bankments built of railroad ties. "There is
enormous *chance* in golf," Haultain writes.
"There must be, when you propel a cubic
inch of gutta-percha over the acres of soil."
His confidence that golf courses will never
become billiard tables and that chance will
healthily affect even the proficient player
might be shaken by what bulldozers and
sprinkler systems have imposed upon
patches of the American wilderness. Modern rules, too, conspire against the genial
misrule of chance. The average golfer
nowadays will not accept a lie in a fairway
divot any more than he accepts one on a
sprinkler head; and "winter rules" infor-
mally obtain even through the lushness of
July. Haultain tells of a chivalrous young
lady who cleaned the mud off her opponent's ball on the green; this tale loses point
when everyone legally picks up and cleans
the ball on the green. Quite often we see, on

the televised tournaments, the ball marked and dusted for the second putt as well, which is carrying the war against chance to the microscopic level. Money and the masses—" 'Arry and 'Arriet," as the class-conscious author puts it—have certainly had their leveling effects upon the game of stalwart Man versus rugged Nature that Haultain so loftily depicts.

Golf's innocent heart, however—the lively tugging between the "motor" and "ideational" centers that occurs when we set ourselves, club in hands, over the ball—remains unchanged, along with the soaring flight of a well-struck shot and the welcome rattle of a purposefully executed putt. Haultain introduces the term "kinæsthesis" to denote the portion of the sport that in the end must be relegated to "feel," to intuition of a deep physical kind, and also to suggest the portion of our pleasure that relates to the unparalleled (except in riflery) amounts of space with which a golfer must contend. The variety of strokes, from the forward-bounding drive to the backward-skipping sand wedge, plus all the improvised punches and cuts that our mortal straying forces upon us, composes one of the game's inexhaustible charms. But Haultain says it best:

> In golf you get the whole gamut of the muscular sense, from the gigantic swipe at the tee to the gentle tap on the green. It is called into play at every stroke, and it differs with every difference of club— its weight, its length of shaft, the angle which its face subtends to the horizon, its rigidity or flexibility, the construction and material of its head. — Golf, in short, is a sort of Gargantuan jugglery, a prodigious prestidigitation, a Titanic thimble-rigging, a mighty legerdemain.

For all its sober, relentless numerical aspect, golf affords the player magical sensations, under the skies, amid the magnitudes of space and chance, and this, its curious central ecstasy, has never been more thoughtfully addressed than in these pages composed by an erudite Canadian tyro when the game was a relative newcomer to our continent. Amid the torrents of writing that have entertained golfers since, Haultain's essay retains the freshness of a mountain spring.